THE
BLACK
PAPERS

THE
BLACK
PAPERS

AN EXPLORATION OF THE DILEMMA WITHIN THE AFRICAN-AMERICAN COMMUNITY

Attallah Ali, Ph.D.

authorHOUSE®

AuthorHouse™
1663 Liberty Drive
Bloomington, IN 47403
www.authorhouse.com
Phone: 1-800-839-8640

Published by AuthorHouse   03/15/2013

ISBN: 978-1-4685-9489-8 (sc)
ISBN: 978-1-4685-9490-4 (hc)
ISBN: 978-1-4685-9491-1 (e)

Library of Congress Control Number: 2012907336

CONTENTS

Dedication

This book is dedicated to the memory of Trayvon Martin, a seventeen-year old African-American teenager who was murdered on February 26, 2012 by George Zimmerman, a White man in Sanford, Florida.

As Trayvon walked home from the store carrying candy and a beverage, George, an exonerated felon stalked and preyed upon him simply because he was Black.

To date, George was arrested on April 11, 2012 six weeks after the murder and was released on $150,000.00 bail ($15,000.00 bond). On June 3_{rd} he surrendered himself to the courts after his bail was revoked for failure to disclose that he received $135,000.00 in donations. Once again, the system of justice has failed the Black community, so it is our right and our duty to protect our children "by any means necessary."

Peace Trayvon!

Special Thanks

Black Women Against Racism Empowered—BWARE

Noel Leader and 100 Blacks in Law Enforcement Who Care

Kwame Goodwin

Barbara Green

Dr. Rasbury

Winona Baca, MA

Viola Plummer and December 12th

William Steen

Kamal

Agnes Johnson

Mia Cruz

Shaka Shakur and the New Black Panther Party—NYC

Sister Kadijah

Delacy Davis

Rafeek and the members of Uhuru

Samuel Lee and Tony Lee—Technology Resource Center, NJ

Black people have adopted a culture that has been harmful
to the growth and development of the Black community. The
abandonment of the "village" mentality has devastated our families
and crippled an entire generation of Black youth.

LET'S GET IT TOGETHER!

PROLOGUE

Racism can be defined as the practice to deny equal opportunities based on race, which hinders a group's ability to thrive and prosper. Although Whites are outnumbered by people of color in a global sense (Ball, 1998) they utilize their influence to dominate the lives of non-Whites—particularly Blacks in the United States of America.

The information presented is based on the premise that the North American Slave Trade forever altered the way in which African-American people would view themselves and others. This atrocity stifled their ability to progress through self-determination and pride. This would interfere with the way Blacks live, socialize, and patronize one another after the civil rights movement as they began to assimilate into the dominate culture.

Black people are more disconnected than ever before. As other groups are organizing their neighborhoods by creating schools and businesses, Black folks are focusing on "how best to keep up with White folks" while ignoring the needs of their own community, particularly their children.

This dilemma is challenging as Black people from around the world consider the United States their home. Many non-African-American Blacks assimilate to that of White America feeling no connection to African-Americans. They have no interest in our history and don't acknowledge the struggles of those before them who have enabled their opportunities for professional and educational growth. Their skewed perception leads them to believe that African-Americans are to blame for their own oppressive state so they are not interested in the formation of a united front to fight racial discrimination. Many non-African-American Black folks are unaware of the laws of racism within the United States of America—Black is Black regardless from which country or island one has arrived. When a racist (judge, doctor, teacher, or neighbor) sees a Black man, he's not going to say "oh that gentleman is from Jamaica." He's going to say "there's another nigger!"

The passive African-American coupled with the ignorant non-African-American Black in a White racist society is a cocktail for disaster and the blame for the collapse of a people.

For centuries Black people have been observed, analyzed, and experimented upon by White intellectuals. It was the color of one's skin that granted him/her eligibility as a specimen. William Shockley, who in 1956 won the Nobel Peace Prize in physics, theorized that Blacks were inherently "less intelligent than Whites." He argued that the government should pay for "less desirables" to be sterilized rather than pay for welfare and other social programs. According to John Hope Franklin (1993) one scholar, Samuel C. Cartwright, compared the learning capacity of an adult Negro to that of a White infant. In the 1994 *The Bell Curve* written by Richard Herrnstein and Charles Murray caused great controversy as the authors asserted that African-Americans were intellectually inferior to other groups. Finally, In September 2005, Bill Bennett, former Secretary of Education, suggested the following on his morning radio show:

> "But I do know that it's true if you want to reduce crime, you could—if that were your *sole* purpose, you could abort every Black baby in this country, and your crime rate would go down. That would be an *impossible, ridiculous, and morally* reprehensible thing to do, but your crime rate would go down. So these far-out, these far-reaching, extensive extrapolations are, I think tricky."

Black people have always been, and will continue to be the scapegoats for all that has gone wrong with the "greatest nation" on earth, even though we have always been denied access to those resources required to cause havoc.

Although the practice to "abort every Black baby" has not yet occurred, the symbolic castration of the Black man continues to be the focus of the political social system in the United States. Bennett's Nazi-like suggestion caused no uproar in the Black community. In fact, Black Women Against Racism and several other grassroots organizations attempted to spearhead a boycott of those advertisers on Bennett's radio show, but "the head negro" in charge from New York City obstructed their efforts.

The increase in foreigners and illegal residents also contributes to the plight of African-Americans. Upon their arrival on American soil, they instantly adopt a stereo-typical view of Black people. An Egyptian woman once told me that when she arrived in the States nine years ago, she was warned by an administrator at the consulate's office to "stay away from the Blacks because they are trouble." Those from other countries rely on the media to define the social/racial climate of the country without understanding the history upon which it developed.

The institution of racism has also had a devastating impact on Black children within the school system. In many cases they are not provided equal educational opportunities as their White counterparts nor are they given an accurate image of historical events that are relevant to the lives of African-Americans. The United States was built on the backs of African-American people, at the hands of White Americans. Those same jobs that Mexican immigrants are now paid for in most cities around the country were once worked by African-American slaves—free of charge.

Sadly, the situation that African-American people have faced has contributed to the break-down of our families and we now live in crisis. Not only are poor people at a disadvantage, but also many who considered themselves "middle-class" have become members of the "working- poor."

While the memory of Africans chained together like cattle will continue to haunt us, it will be the bondage of their minds and souls that will eventually result in their destruction, the ultimate mission of the White slave master. The Black intellectuals on whom we so desperately rely on for support are so concerned with assimilating into the dominant culture that they are uninvolved in making improvements in our community.

The Black Papers are meant to stimulate thought provoking conversation with the hope that Black people will stand up, speak-up, and not wait for the "slave master" or a "leading Black point person" selected by the media to guide the way. It is that leading Black point person who will lead us back into slavery.

It is my goal to inspire others to understand the connection of our tragic history to our current state of madness through a review of important historical events. I will examine those areas within the Black community that I believe have contributed to the Black dilemma. Only then will we be able to take responsibility and help ourselves so that we will be able to move forward and create a solid foundation for Black children.

This book provides an overview of the subject matter in addition to my experiences as an African-American woman and single mother of two sons and a daughter. My contributions as an Activist, Psychologist, and Educator in the New York Metropolitan area have enabled me to connect with Black people from various parts of the United States. I will share my experiences but not debate them. My journey will be narrated from my perspective. John Hope Franklin (1993) states "I venture to state categorically that the problem of the twenty-first century will be the problem of the color line. This conclusion arises from the fact that by any standard of measurement or evaluation the problem has not been resolved in the twentieth century, and this becomes a part of the legacy and burden of the next century" (p. 5). The descriptions "African-American" and "Black" will be used in different context. African-American will be used to describe those Africans brought to the United States by way of the North American slave trade. The description "Black" will be used when making reference to all non-Hispanic Black people.

TROUBLED WATERS

"The Black world of America is unlike the White
in more ways than mere color."
Harold Cruise—Author

Where better to begin then with the conspiracy in New Orleans, Louisiana, known as Hurricane Katrina. I began writing this manuscript in July 2005 before the devastation of Katrina. While I was cognizant of our lack of cohesiveness prior to this tragedy, it was the loss of over 1500 of my people and the suffering of 1000 others that would provide me a knowledge base to understand better the scope of our plight.

This disaster would confirm my belief that Black life in the United States of America is disposable—like trash—and that those Blacks in positions of power have opted to ignore acts of injustice because they have sold themselves to the establishment and do not want to jeopardize their own livelihood. This is often true for Black leaders as well as for some athletes, entertainers, and other affluent Black folks. Such an approach is reminiscent of the "house negro" during slavery.

Those who would survive the deadly flood were forced to watch loved ones drown in their homes. They would be left to fend for themselves without assistance from the local government, federal government, or from those Black folks with the means to help. It was clear that reporters made a conscious effort to tell only stories of "White on Black heroism" even if there were stories of Black folks saving their own. Sadly, as an avid listener of Black radio, I heard very little about our "Black well-to-do negroes" assisting in the aftermath of this tragedy. What has happened to us? How is it that we have more multi-millionaires than ever before and we don't find it necessary to help those less fortunate? Is it that we don't have the power to demand certain rights for our people? If that's so, then we have not really made it, have we? Was there no way that Black entertainers or athletes could have pooled their resources and leased a plane or helicopter to send food or water to those in need? How could we sit and watch from our homes as other Black people begged for help while they held their dying newborn babies and their ailing elderly parents? We didn't even protest when our Black men were killed at the hands of law enforcement as they entered abandoned stores to find food for their families.

There were rumors that the natural disaster was not a disaster after all, but rather a conspiracy to flood New Orleans. This assertion focuses on the fact that the devastation was not caused by the hurricane itself but by the failure of the damaged levees. The failure of the levees coincided with the re-gentrification of Black neighborhoods in many major cities in the country. When White folks are ready to move into a community, they move Black folks out—and as always, we succumb to the demands of Master. The projects in New Orleans that housed thousand of socially and economically deprived people have been replaced with townhomes and gated communities for upper-middle class Whites.

The conspiracy to displace and kill thousands of Black people from New Orleans is in accordance with both the history and the current trends of this country. When members of the White establishment decide to relocate to a specific region, they do so with great power. We have witnessed these "takeovers" in many major cities around the country, including Harlem, New York, one of the most meaningful places in the country for Black people. Harold Cruise (1984) describes Harlem as:

> "The most important community of Black America . . . the Black world's quest for identity and salvation. The way in which Harlem goes (or does not go) so goes all of Black America." (p. 12)

We now know that Harlem no longer belongs to Black folks. The neighborhood in which our people organized politically, economically, and culturally has a new face. Unfortunately, this happened at the hands of Black leaders who "sold out." The lack of supportive response by Blacks in a financial position to assist is symbolic of our community. Immediately following Hurricane Katrina, Lil Wayne, Kanye West, Will I Am , and very few other entertainers donated time and money to the victims. Of course many others soon jumped on the bandwagon when they realized that they wouldn't be whipped by "slave master." I was forced to listen to reports that follow the efforts of entertainers such as Brad Pitt and Harry Connick Jr. who had donated their time and resources to assist in the rebuilding of the ninth ward—an area of New Orleans most devastated by the flood.

In the documentary by Spike Lee, *When the Levee Breaks* (2006), one resident spoke of the plan to bring in immigrants to plant trees and assist in the rebuilding of New Orleans. He went on to say how the establishment wouldn't even allow Black men from the neighborhood to contribute their skills. What better way to instill a sense of pride and ownership? This would have been the perfect opportunity to provide this disenfranchised group with a sense of hope—to break the cycle of helplessness among those from low-income neighborhoods by enabling them to participate in the rebuilding of their own homes. Instead, we want to deny Black men (once again) of their manhood and their ability to provide for their families. We then wonder why some are so enraged that they resort to activities that are considered criminal with no sense of commitment to family. Such feelings of inferiority coupled with the loss of the "village mentality" create a lethal combination.

At some time during the last thirty-five or so years, we decided to adopt the cultural practices of White-Americans, and these are often in direct conflict with our identity as African people. White America's greedy fixation on "power at any expense" and the choice to raise their children without guidelines or boundaries is not representative of who we are and from where we originated. According to Dr. Joy DeGruy, during an interview with Gil Noble on *Like It Is* family and ancestral lines are crucial to West African culture from where many African-Americans have come. Our men are warriors by nature who protect their women and children. Unfortunately, the White establishment has redefined their role for them, and Black men have therefore lost much of their heritage and direction.

While it is clear that the White establishment has interfered with the continuous progression of the Black community, we must also begin to self-reflect and acknowledge the fact that we have been our own worst enemy, as many of us suffer from "Post-Traumatic Slave Disorder" as coined by Dr. Joy DeGruy. We are so wounded that we cannot see the value in ourselves. We have a hatred of self that has been passed down from one generation to the next. This self-hatred hampers our ability to support one another in a time of need—such as an event as devastating as Hurricane Katrina.

Six years later—upon the completion of this book—there have been no marked improvements as related to the unification of Black people. Even the election of our first Black President has caused a great divide among us.

SLAVERY, POST-SLAVERY, AND THE BLACK COMMUNITY

"To protect the sheep you have to catch the wolf.
Only a wolf can catch a wolf."
Marcus Garvey—Activist

Slavery

The United States of America would not be the most powerful country in the world if it were not for the contributions of African-American slaves. While European slave owners may have developed the social and economical infrastructure as stolen from the Native Americans, it would be the hard labor of slaves who would actually build the country with no financial compensation or recognition.

The enslavement of Africans began as early as 1441 at the hands of Antonio Gonzales, a navigator from Portugal who gave twelve Africans to the King of Portugal. Portugal had a stake in the European slave trade, and this had a great impact on the economy (Civil Rights Chronicle, 2003). It began with an interest in the goods to which Africans had access: gold, spices, and ivory. Eventually, they (Africans) became most valuable as they could be traded for a profit that would be used to purchase New World materials such as sugar, tobacco, and coffee.

The African-American slave trade began around 1650. Africans were chained together in tight, hot, dark quarters for months at a time. Some died from disease and were left chained to the others. Upon arrival at the slave ports in cities such as Jamestown, Philadelphia, Richmond, Charleston and New Orleans, families were torn apart as men were sent off to one plantation while their wives and children were sent to another. This began the division of the African-American family, a phenomenon that would ultimately decimate our successful progress as a people. According to Blassingame (1979)

> "The process of enslavement was almost unbelievably painful and bewildering for the Africans. Completely cut off from their native land, they were frightened by the artifacts of the White man's civilization and terrified by his cruelty." (p. 4)

Blassingame went on to report that most of the slaves captured were from West Africa and were used to perform hard labor. Approximately ten million Africans were brought to the New World between the sixteenth and the nineteenth centuries.

Slaves could not understand the language of their masters nor could they understand the language of one another, as they were from different parts of Africa. It was typical for those from the same tribe to be separated to safeguard against rebellion. Another practice of the slave-owner was to prohibit the unsupervised gathering of more than a few slaves for fear of their organizing and attacking the slave owners. This feeling of helplessness holds true today in the workplace, as many of my friends and colleagues across the country have admitted that their White employer oftentimes appears uncomfortable if more than two Black employees are gathered together whether conversing about business or otherwise.

Enslaved Africans not only endured harsh physical abuse but also they lost their self-respect and sense of independence. Eventually, the slave became dependent on his master. Slave owners devised a system that was abusive not only physically but also psychologically. Educators, journalists, and politicians described the Negro as a beast that drained the economy and threatened humanity. It was common for the slave master to rape his female slaves—a reminder to the Black male that he was in no position to protect the most valued treasure in his life. Another practice that interfered with the development of unity among Africans was to separate them according to the color of their skin. Those with lighter skin were given jobs indoors, working as nannies and housekeepers, while those who were darker had to work in the fields. This focus on skin color would continue to divide the Black community long after slavery ended.

Post Slavery

Unlike the Jews and the aftermath of the Holocaust, African-Americans were never able to organize and move forward with force. When slaves were emancipated, they were sent away empty-handed without the economic means to provide for their family, without friends and without land to stand upon. When the Hebrews were emancipated, they were given three acres of ground upon which they could live and make a living (Frederick Douglas). According to Hughes and Meltzer (1983) emancipated Blacks were homeless. They roamed the Southern roads like gypsies. Eventually, the former slaves began to migrate to the North and West in search of a new life as freed slaves. They would join other Blacks who had lived as free people in many large cities across the country. At the time slavery ended, 4.4 million of the population was Black (14% of the population) with only 488,000 men and women having lived as "free" citizens.

The Jim Crow laws would ultimately result in the creation of a more cohesive Black community. Jim Crow refers to a form of segregation that forbade Black people from frequenting the same places as Whites, as Blacks were considered "animal-like." Jim Crow was a term taken from a song performed by a White minstrel entertainer in 1830. The entertainer blackened his face and behaved as though he were a bumbling Black man.

Jim Crow became the term to describe segregation in the South through the 1960's, even though this practice was not restricted to the South. Black people who migrated to large cities in the North were forced into their own communities as they were not permitted to live among White residents. This resulted in the development of Black-owned stores, banks, barber shops, medical practices, schools and restaurants. Black people were self-sufficient because they had no choice but to be so. According to Carter G. Woodson (1999), "Above all things, the effort must result in making a man think and do for himself just as the Jews have done in spite of universal persecution." (p. 10)

Racial segregation was their reality, and Black families created ties to one another as though they were related. There was a sense of unity, but they felt that the laws of segregation interfered with their access to the same services as their White counterparts. But rather than fight for separate but equal, they began to fight for the right to be included in social, business and educational settings with White people, even though Whites expressed feelings of outrage at the thought of interacting with Blacks. So began the Civil Rights Movement.

The Civil Rights Movement

This movement began to build in the 1950's while Jim Crow was still alive. Black people began to unite on a new front—the right to equal treatment in a country built by their forefathers. While the number of tragic events and lives lost during this struggle are essentially innumerable, there are several milestones that have affected the direction of the movement. Bell Hooks (1995) reminds us of the many events throughout history in which Black folks defended themselves against the assault of White people by killing their attackers in self-defense. She goes on to say that "Black rage" is not accepted while unprovoked rage, fueled by hatred at the hand of White people is.

Carson (2003) provides a time-line of events that were significant to the Civil Rights Movement.

- 1954. Brown vs. Board of Education. The ruling mandated the racial integration of public schools.
- 1955. Emmett Till, age 14, was murdered by the brother and husband of a White woman whom Emmett called "baby" when leaving a store. The men gouged out an eye and crushed his skull. Emmett's mother demanded that the casket be left open during viewing so visitors and the media could see "the face of hatred." Both men were found "not guilty" but the event became the topic of discussion internationally. The United

States lost its prestige abroad and this supported the growth of the civil rights movement.

- 1955. Rosa Parks refuses to give up her seat on a bus in Montgomery Alabama so that a White man could sit down. This resulted in a "bus boycott" that would continue for one year. People carpooled and walked rather than use public transportation. The year-long protest ended with a U.S. Supreme Court ruling that declared public bus segregation unconstitutional.
- 1957. Civil Rights Act of 1957. This ruling secured a division within the Justice Department which would protect the civil rights of all citizens and grant the federal government the right to charge legally anyone who interferes with one's right to vote. Nine Black students known as "the Little Rock Nine" integrated Central High School in Little Rock, Arkansas. The students were escorted by federal troops as an angry mob of White protestors called for their lynching.
- 1960. Adam Clayton Powell, Jr. began to mobilize the people in Harlem. This was important, as Harlem was the place to which Black people and others looked for Black culture and the overall Black experience.
- 1960. Students organized a "sit-in" at Woolworth's department store in Greensboro North Carolina. This movement encouraged leadership by women, youth and poor people.
- 1960. Citizens of Birmingham Alabama demonstrated and were attacked by dogs and police with water hose.
- 1961. Atlanta's Black college students began to take a leadership role in the Civil Rights movement as they grew tired of the lack of effectiveness of older leaders. They chose a popular White-owned department store to boycott. Atlanta's "old guard" Black leaders tried to interfere in the process.
- 1963. Dr. Martin Luther King, Jr. delivered his speech, "I Have a Dream," at the march on Washington.
- 1964. James Powell, 15 years old, was killed by White police officers in Harlem. Two days later, a crowd gathered outside the police station and demanded that the officers be arrested for murder.

- 1965. The Voting Rights Act is reinforced and a bill is signed by President Johnson.
- 1965. Civil Rights activist Malcolm X is assassinated in New York City while making a speech.
- 1966. Stokely Carmichael, executive director of SNCC, issued a call for Black power. Bobby Seale and Huey Newton formed the Black Panther Party for Self Defense in Oakland, California.
- 1967. Summer riots in Newark, New Jersey, Detroit, New York, Chicago, Cleveland, Washington and Atlanta sparked confrontations with police.
- 1967. U.S. Solicitor General Thurgood Marshall is appointed to the Supreme Court as the nation's first Black to serve in this capacity.
- 1968. Poor People's Campaign organized a march to Washington. Martin Luther King, Jr., believed that while the basic needs of Black people had been taken care of by law, most Blacks were poor and that interfered with their quality of life. King announced that poor people would march for jobs and demanded the formation of a bill that would protect them. In the midst of the planning process, Dr. King was assassinated. Rev. Ralph Abernathy and others led the march.
- 1969. Black college students began to demand more Black studies programs at various universities and historically Black colleges.
- 1970.'s. " Black Power Movement" began to build. Men and women sported natural hair. More Blacks gained political power as Blacks were supportive of one another. Racist Whites were punished for hate crimes against and murders of Blacks pre-civil rights; i.e., Robert Chambers was found guilty of first degree murder for the 1963 bombing of the 16_{th} Street church in which four little girls were killed.

It appeared that the 1970's was the beginning of a new era for the Black community. One would think that the combination of political presence and cohesive community would enable Black folks an opportunity of self-determination and wealth. This was not the case. The 70's would be the peak of the "Black Power Movement" before its demise. Black people began to operate as though they were victorious against the institution of racism. They began to feel a sense of false security as Whites permitted them to work with them, move into their neighborhoods, and populate their schools, not realizing that as the Blacks were moving in, White people were moving out. Howard Ball (1998) states the following:

> "Although vastly outnumbered by the colored peoples of the world, Whites used their power and technology ruthlessly to dominate non-Whites, particularly in America, where African-Americans were worse off than impoverished serfs of some federal kingdom." (p.1)

Post Civil Rights

By the mid 1980's, half of all Black students would still attend schools that were segregated and inferior to those schools available to their White counterparts. The practice known as "White flight" would now become the tool to segregate the nation. In reality, Black people had not progressed beyond where they had been two decades earlier. The difference was that overt acts of racial violence had been replaced with racism that was more subtle. The White establishment was diligent in its practice to stifle the growth and development of the Black community. They were concerned that the unification of Black people would promote within the Black community a sense of self worth and respect, vital to the survival of any race of people.

Most recently, a discussion on the remains of slaves found in New York City has stimulated much discussion among Black folks. According to Dr. Joy DeGruy, the bones that were discovered rewrote history. Most discussions on slavery in textbooks tend to focus on the southern region of the country, when in fact all thirteen colonies participated in the slave trade. Dr. DeGruy went on to say that White folks have not participated in a media frenzy over the discovery because then they would be required to change the history books in our schools to reflect the truth rather than to continue to present a fabricated story about the inhumane treatment of Black people. She goes on to ask, "What would happen if little White boys and girls understood the truth? That Black people were chained and treated like animals? What would happen if Black children understood? White folks will continue to suppress the truth as it pertains to slavery because if they expose the truth about us then they are exposed as well."

Nevertheless, cohesiveness among Black people has never fully materialized. Black people have lost the drive to fight for equality. Many believe that their "suburban status" is synonymous with "social success" when in fact the practice of institutional racism is present in every facet of their lives. The force once known as "the Black community" no longer demonstrates the strength exhibited pre-Civil Rights. New Orleans, like Harlem, New York, represented Black talent and intellectual growth during the 1900's. The choice to abandon the "village mentality" has interfered with our sense of Black pride and cohesiveness. We no longer feel the need to advocate for our children or protect our elders. Most damaging is that White folks are aware of this disconnect and use it to their advantage.

BLACK LEADERSHIP

"A sellout is a person who betrays something to which he
is said to owe allegiance. When used in a racial context
among African-Americans, sellout is a disparaging term
that refers
to Blacks who knowingly or with gross negligence act
against the interest of Blacks as a whole."
Randall Kennedy—Author

I knew on August 31, 2005, after our "leading Blacks" failed to respond to the tragedy of Hurricane Katrina that we were in trouble. I remember asking, "Where is everyone?" One would have thought that the "leaders" would have organized a call-to-action and SHUT THIS COUNTRY DOWN! When that didn't happen, I began to think about my children growing-up in a country where people who look like them have no concern for their future.

Why are Black people one of the only groups that wait for a point person to express feelings of anger when they are discriminated against? Are we so afraid of the White establishment that we have to hide behind the rhetoric of those "leading Blacks" who appear to advocate for our rights? Are we so naïve that we believe that the "leading Blacks" selected by the media and members from the establishment themselves are going to fight for social and racial change? Why don't we speak for ourselves and our families? We have placed television and radio talk-show-hosts in the position of "leader" even though they do not have the capacity to serve as such, since they are bound by contracts and agreements with advertisers and cannot advocate for the Black community in a way that would be effective.

Sixty years ago Black people were in need of a spokesperson to speak out against the inhumane treatment they had to endure. While there were thousands of men and women who died fighting for civil rights of Black people, Malcolm X and Dr. Martin Luther King, Jr., would organize the Black community in a way never experienced before in American history. According to Manning Marable (2011), Dr. King was associated with small Southern towns, while Malcolm X represented Black folks in the inner city ghettos. He was a man of uncompromising action who could not be bought in any way—the polar opposite of the leading Blacks who represent us today. The time warranted such leadership, but as we move through the twenty-first century we must adopt a modified version of infiltrating the institution of racism as it affects Black people and this requires the work of many "soldiers" as opposed to one chief. This requires a grassroots approach to politics which must involve the working class and the economically deprived.

The Sellout

Most of the leaders of today (leading Blacks) are fraudulent. They talk the talk but don't walk the walk. They deceive the masses by organizing occasional demonstrations at which they will stage a scene, causing them to be arrested and led away in handcuffs. This is to divert the attention of the people. The motive of the leading Black (sellout) is to be offered a seat at the bargaining table by members of the establishment. It's safe to say that there are several "leading Blacks" as selected by the White establishment who fit the description of a "sellout." Instead of Malcolm X we have Al Sharpton. Instead of Dr. King we have Calvin Butts. And instead of Adam Clayton Powell Jr. we have Charles Rangle. None of these "leading Blacks" are concerned genuinely about the progression of Black people. Harold Cruise (1984) suggested the following:

> "The young generation must first clear the way to cultural revolution by a critical assault on the methods and ideology of the old-guard negro intellectual elite." (p. 99)

Cruise goes on to report that their shortcomings have interfered with the ability to motivate the Black masses.

The Elders

One major problem within the realm of Black leadership is the failure of our elder leaders to step aside. Many of them are older men who insist on implementing an approach of activism that is no longer effective against the form of racism that exists currently. Racism 21C (twenty first century) is gangster. Rather than hanging Black men and women from trees at the same frequency as during the 1960's, Whites have flooded our neighborhoods with illicit drugs, resulting in Black-on-Black crime and murder. They torture psychologically our children in school and on the streets, hammering their self-confidence, causing great distress to their level of self confidence and their will to thrive. This conspiracy is not localized to the inner-city. Black children (particularly boys) from anywhere USA are targets. How best to destroy a people but through their children. Unfortunately, the "good old Black boy network" is not interested in establishing a method to deal with this new and more potent form of racism, but rather concerned with creating a platform to promote themselves—in other words, dancing for dinner.

After Sean Bell was murdered by several members of the NYPD, the number-one "leading Black," Al Sharpton, organized a town hall meeting in which he requested the attendance of all Black activists. During this meeting, he made a statement in front of an estimated 150 Black leaders and activists that any plan agreed upon could not fail, for failure would suggest weakness. Such a message is harmful to members within our community as we already suffer from low self-esteem and disbelief in our own ability to be effective. We need to remember that there can be **no** success without failure.

Most suggestions by the many Black female activists were dismissed. For instance, during the same meeting, a well-known female activist and politician questioned the plans for a holiday protest. She asked, "How should we ask the participants to get to the site? Public transportation or car?" Sharpton replied, "However you women would get to Tiffany's to go shopping is how you should arrive."

During the meeting, the women of BWARE suggested "holiday boycotts" which would include Easter and Mother's Day Shopping. Sharpton said "what does that have to do with fighting the system?" As if he didn't know. He and the other members of his team eventually agreed with our proposal only because the other leaders who were present understood the relevance and they would have questioned his refusal. The idea was to boycott Mother's Day purchases from department stores and other retail outlets around the city.

Over the course of several weeks and many planning meetings, leaders organized venues in which we could meet and plan. One minister offered his church as a starting point of the event in Brooklyn. Skeptical, I believed that there were police informants and other agents invited to these events. We, the members of BWARE, were careful with our information.

On Mother's Day as the participants arrived at the site in Brooklyn as instructed, they were told by the minister's assistant that they could not organize in front of his church. They were told that his church was not to be involved in the boycott. While this was a disappointment, it was not a surprise. Our elders are at their end. They have sold out and will continue to do so at the expense of the rest of the Black community.

After the march, I stood in a subway car with a male colleague. He became overly excited as he recognized a well-known Black scholar and activist, James Smalls. Excitedly he asked "Attallah, do you know who that is?" When I responded "No," he said, "That's James Smalls!" I said, "Ok." He immediately motioned for me to follow him so that he could introduce himself and me to this "Mr. Smalls." My colleague went on to explain to Mr. Smalls that I was the President of BWARE (Black Women Against Racism Empowered). Mr. Smalls began to question my approach to dealing with racism. As I explained that we are interested in empowering members from the African-American community through activism and involvement in their own neighborhoods, he began to explain to me why my focus was wrong. I was not impressed with his advice and went on to inform him that all can contribute in their own way, as long as they contribute. He asked "What's your name? Attallah? You look like Attallah and have a fresh mouth like Attallah . . . Shabazz that is." (Attallah Shabazz is the daughter of Malcolm X).

After this draining one-way conversation, I informed my male colleague that I was not impressed by a person simply because of their titles and past accomplishments if they are no longer effective. I find that we often pay homage to those elders who may have contributed a decade ago but have either sold out or interfered with the progression and growth of a "strong Black community."

The disrespect towards Black female activists by their male counterparts illustrates the sad reality that sexism is alive within the movement. Many of our male leaders are opposed to the views and opinions of women as related to the racism within our community, and they belittle their efforts and contributions.

Many of these men have become addicted to the camera, resulting in them selling their souls to the devil for a chance at fame. Sadly, our youth are suffering, as there has been no one to show them the way. The Civil Rights movement was organized by young adults, not by senior citizens. The role of our elders is to show us the way then we are responsible for getting there.

In the fall of 2009, I was invited by my sons' (ages 9 and 12) football coach to speak to members of the local recreational football team in Paterson, New Jersey. The topic of discussion was "how to be the best person that you can be." It was decided that I would discuss "Respecting Black Women." As I prepared for the presentation, I began to focus on racism and respect for self. While I understood clearly the need for our young Black boys to respect their female counterparts, I felt that I had much more to share with them. In fact, my philosophical belief has always been that our young Black girls and women are treated in the manner that they allow boys/men to treat them. I felt as though I needed to speak to the girls first.

As the lecture began, I noticed that I was the only female speaker. The facilitator was excited as he introduced speaker after speaker by their titles—Rev. Brown, Dr. Anderson, and Professor Jones. As the men spoke, some of the younger children became restless. Immediately, the facilitator rushed to the floor and began to discipline the boys and demanded that they be respectful while "the brother" was speaking. Afterwards, I was introduced as "Miss Ali." I had to reintroduce myself as "Dr. Ali." I began with a history lesson so that the children understood that they came from greatness—kings and queens in Africa. After I had their attention for ten minutes or so, I began to lose the younger boys. As they began to move around and talk, my male counterparts stood directly behind me and did not intervene. The children were so loud that I had to stop and remind my "brothers" that this was their opportunity to show our boys how to be respectful of women. Hurt and ashamed of my "Black men," I realized that this is a microcosm of real life. These men were not supportive of me or my views. How could they expect our children to be so?

New York City

New York City is the center of the universe, the most powerful city in the world, and home to the best and the brightest minds. Historically speaking, Harlem, New York was the base from which dynamic leadership and activism was bred. Leaders such as Adam Clayton Powell, Jr. and Malcolm X. One would believe that Black pride would dominate the streets. What better place to set an example for the rest of the country to follow? Where better to organize and fight against police brutality? There are probably more intellectual brothers and sisters here than anywhere else in the world. So why isn't New York the symbol of Black strength? Plainly stated, many of us are suffering from Post Traumatic Slave Disorder, a condition described by Dr. Joy DeGruy.

The people of New York have been bamboozled. Many have allowed the leading Blacks to destroy continually the strength and power of the committed advocates as they use their positions to take over and then extinguish effective methods to deal with an act or crime of hate directed against the Black community. These are some of the events in question:

- Several years ago, the *New York Post* came under fire for printing a cartoon image of a chimpanzee that was shot by two White police officers who made references to it as President Obama. Sharpton put Black folks in a frenzy, as he called for a boycott of the *Post*. He then called for a demonstration in front of the *Post* headquarters. He led a rally, in which participants marched up and down within a barricaded area like cattle. This was a planned event, held with the permission of the NYPD. One week later, the fire was out and there was no more talk of protest or boycott.

- Don Imus, radio talk show host, described the young women on the Rutgers University basketball team as "nappy-headed hos." Members from grassroots organizations and professional Black groups demanded that Imus be fired or an economic boycott would ensue. This seemed to be the moment—Black folks were angry and tired of the continued racism that plagued members of the Black community. But then what happened? Our leading Black positioned himself and his posse at the helm of the controversy, insisting that "Imus be fired" but then changing his tune stating that "Imus deserved the right to work." The controversy ended and Imus eventually resurfaced on the airwaves.

  Similarly, in 2012, a White female student from Georgetown University spoke publically in favor of insurance companies including the cost of birth control pills under a woman's health plan. Talk show host Rush Limbaugh fired back and called the student a slut. Liberal groups organized and were able to pressure twelve advertisers to remove their ads from his show.

- In November 2006, Sean Bell was murdered by members of the NYPD. Once again, the Black community was prepared to do whatever was needed to address the issue of police brutality and murder within our community. Several leading Blacks (including clergy and politicians) organized a leadership meeting so that activists within the Black community could express their ideas as to how best to deal with the tragedy. An economic boycott and a series of demonstrations were suggested, as it was the holiday season—what better way to make a statement than to interfere with Christmas in New York? Unfortunately, our "leading Black" led us nowhere but back to the plantations. The head Negro in charge once again rallied the troops but did nothing with them. There was no follow-up meeting to initiate the boycott.

In each situation, the masses were prepared to move forward in whatever direction would result in appropriate consequences for the perpetrator; but somewhere during the process, the leading Blacks shut it down. We must not permit the "ambulance chasers and spotlight seekers" to use those events that degrade the lives of Black people as vehicles for their own personal agendas. Failure to intervene will result in continued brutalization of Black people at the hands of the police.

Black Organizations

The function of the Black organization is to address the needs of Black people as related to issues of racism. To date, most major cities in the country are home to various organizations that advocate for these rights. Some are grassroots efforts populated by "the people," while others are more organized and consist of professional Black folks.

My experience as an activist has been that those groups formed by the people have been most effective. Those Black organizations led by professionals tend to advocate through debates and long-winded rhetoric. They usually present their arguments to one another rather than to the White establishment.

NAACP

In the past, when one thought of a community based organization, The National Association of the Advancement of Colored People (or the NAACP) would come to mind; however, their power and effectiveness pre-civil rights, exists no more. They no longer assist people; instead, they hide behind scholarship dinners and membership dues. They are not accessible at the local level to assist Black citizens with issues of racism and discrimination.

This organization had been reduced to a name that can be associated with assimilation. A name which bears the description "colored people" that is no longer appropriate in which to identify Blacks. It almost seems fitting since the NAACP operates under the establishment of which it was organized originally to fight against.

A memorable incident occurred in 2008 when a sixth grade teacher from Caldwell, New Jersey, assigned her students a project in which they were required to be plantation owners. The requirement was that the students had to create an advertisement that would describe why their plantations were profitable. One of the parents of a Black student found the project to be insensitive and reported the story to the media. As several grassroots organizations began to ask that the teacher be terminated, the spokesperson for the New Jersey chapter of the NAACP denounced the request that the teacher be fired and asked only for an apology.

Such a response is typical by the head Negros in charge who behave as gatekeepers. As long as the leading Blacks in decision making positions continue to act as "buffers" when issues of racism arise, we will never be treated with respect.

The National Urban League

Formerly known as the National League on Urban Conditions Among Negros, was formed in 1920 as a civil rights organization. The mission of the group was to advocate for the economical freedom and the civil rights of African-Americans.

To date, the Urban League focuses on gun control, violence, and other issues within the community. It's safe to say that this organization must become more visible and provide more resources and assistance to the Black community.

National Action Network

The mission of this organization is vague. Reverend Al Sharpton seems to play host to the "highest bidder" as leader of this organization. The agency does not focus on the needs of the Black folks who live in the community or communities like it, but rather on how best to strengthen the role of its leader in the national political arena.

Sharpton continues to deceive his followers. His role as "activist" is clearly a ploy to distract people from his incestuous relationship with the White establishment. He is a "gate keeper" chosen by members of the system to diffuse the reaction of the "community" during a "racial crisis." Most often, he organizes a protest to appear as though he is protesting an incident such as racial discrimination or police brutality. This is usually a "march to nowhere" and participants are required to participate in an orderly protest within blocks defined by barricades as organized by the NYPD. During such a spectacle, Sharpton and his entourage stop every so often for a photo opportunity, which may end in a quiet arrest, handcuffs and all. Usually, the protest ends with Sharpton leaving once he reaches the end, without making a statement as his followers walk through the "finish line." At the end of the rally for Sean Bell, five young Black boys stood around for thirty minutes waiting to hear Sharpton or a representative speak. When they realized that there was no effective closure to the rally they set an American flag on fire.

Black Women Against Racism Empowered (BWARE)

This organization began in 1990 as Black Women Against Racism in Education.

The catalyst for this organization was the former Secretary of Education, Bill Bennett, who stated that "the only way to reduce crime in this country is to abort all Black babies." It was clear that the NAACP, Sharpton, and none of our "leading Blacks" were going to respond in a manner that would be effective. Thus a group of sisters from various faiths and socioeconomic backgrounds organized and attacked this situation with strength.

The goal of BWARE is to call for an economic boycott against any corporation that discriminates against members of the Black community. In the case of Bennett, we attacked those companies that advertised on Bennett's show and vowed to "stop the shop" of their product unless they pulled their advertisement off the show. The focus of the boycott was the Disney Company, whose public relation person contacted the president of BWARE to address their concerns that their products, from movies to toys, would be boycotted by the Black community, thus proving the power of the "economic boycott."

BWARE, along with several other grassroots organizations, has gone on to confront racist mistreatment by several educational institutions, retail establishments, nursing homes, media outlets and police departments across the tri-state area.

To date, the women of BWARE have focused their attention on the educational system by acting as advocates for parents dealing with children who have been wrongfully placed in special education classes.

Noel Leader and 100 Blacks In Law Enforcement Who Care

These brothers and sisters *are* New York's finest as they speak openly about police brutality and racial discrimination within the Black community. They take to the streets or courtroom—wherever their advocacy is needed. This approach is effective as they cannot be "bought out" as have many of the leading Blacks.

Comprised of retired police officers and other law enforcement agents, these men and women are committed to improving the lives of Black people. When not confronting "the boys in blue," they volunteer their time to visit schools and mentor at-risk teens or they join forces with other like-minded organizations. In fact, they were the first group to support the efforts of BWARE as they endorsed the group's approach and participated in protests and other plans of action.

The members of 100 Blacks In Law Enforcement epitomize "Black leadership." Their pledge to safeguard the Black community is commendable and much appreciated.

Black Cops Against Police Brutality—BCAP

The founder of BCAP is Delacy Davis, a retired Sergeant from the East Orange Police Department in East Orange, New Jersey. The organization was formed to advocate for victims of police brutality within the tri-state area. However, brother Delacy travels around the world to discuss racism and other social struggles as related to Black people within the United States.

Viola Plummer and December 12th Movement

The December 12th Movement is a Brooklyn-based, grassroots organization founded by Sonny Abubadika Carson in the 60's. The central purpose of the organization is to focus on "self-determination" for Black people and others who are oppressed. Brother Carson's contributions include fighting for community control of schools in the 1960's; and in 1980 he organized and founded Black Men Against Crack. Brother Carson passed away in 2002, but his work continues through the loyalty of those sisters and brothers who support the movement.

Their efforts to advocate for the rights of African people both in America and in Africa do not go unnoticed by those involved in the movement. In September 2008, December 12th organized a protest against police brutality in New York City. The demonstration included thousands of New Yorkers marching through the streets of the financial district during the evening rush hour. This event was free of violence and did not occur with the approval of the NYPD. The crowd impeded traffic for 45 minutes. Motorists were angry and the police frustrated, proving that this had been an effective demonstration.

Viola Plummer and her organization continue to act as leaders in this grassroots movement. They are able to convince their peers to fight for justice by utilizing a pre-civil rights approach—activism uncommon from the contemporary activist.

The Agnes Johnson Movement

This sister and her daughter Mia Cruz have advocated for the rights of Black and Hispanic people in Harlem and the surrounding boroughs for years. Most recently, the duo monitored police activity in midtown Manhattan after many youngsters reported that they were being harassed by the police on their way home from school. When Ms. Johnson and Ms. Cruz witnessed such harassment, they accompanied the young students to the police station and assisted them and their guardians in filing formal complaints against the officers.

Milton Almadi, CEO, The Black Star News

Brother Almadi is serious about his contributions to the Black community. Conscious of the police brutality and harassment towards young Black men in the community, he has requested that anyone who has experienced such behavior at the hands of the NYPD contact his establishment so that he can feature their story.

The New Black Panther Party—New York City

Brother Shaka Shakur, Sister Kadijah, and others have expressed their loyalty in their attempt to improve the quality of life within the Black community. They have focused their efforts on speaking out against police brutality and educating young Black children against drug abuse and other behavior that has interfered with their growth and development. Brother Shaka and his cohorts encourage young children who live in public housing to keep their buildings clean. He organizes a weekly "clean-up" in which children take turns mopping the hallway floors and cleaning the elevators. Such mentoring has a direct impact on the children involved.

Educated Black Folks

Several seasons ago the reality show "Harlem Heights" in which several young educated twenty-something year-old men and women shared their experiences with employment, family, and love on the air. Prior to its viewing, I expected to watch people that I consider to be "real" products of Harlem, not transients who clearly have been brought in from the outside. It was disappointing to watch, as many of the girls spoke in a manner that imitates the language and tone of their White peers. While one or two of the "brothers" spoke of their need to assist with community involvement, the women were more concerned with living their lives as socialites. Do they represent our educated youth? I hope not.

While working on my doctorate I participated in a program organized to pair together Black students who were graduates of historically Black colleges with instructors who also had an affiliation with Black schools as well. During this meeting, each of the professors shared with the group his or her educational background and employment experiences. Their purpose was to provide the students with advice and suggestions on how best to complete the program. Most boasted of their accomplishments instead of sharing helpful information. Once the group session was complete, the students were expected to introduce themselves to those instructors whose expertise was in their field of study. While the Black male instructors were somewhat helpful, the Black female professors were arrogant and unapproachable. They sat in a group and discussed the price of their pocketbooks and jewelry as students attempted to engage them in conversations relevant to their studies. This was a major disappointment to me and would be the first of many encounters with my professional brothers and sisters.

We describe success by evaluating one's financial stability, athletic or artistic accomplishment, educational status, and/or political power. Black people have clearly made their mark in each of these areas, but they still have not gained the respect of the White establishment. All Black people, regardless of economic class, are at risk of being discriminated against or mistreated because of their race; and until we as a people unite, the practice of oppression and hate will continue. The White establishment has a clear understanding of how to divide and conquer within the Black community and the use of economic greed has become the vehicle of choice.

There are those successful Blacks who may be first generation college graduates, including doctors, lawyers, and executives who hold position within a major firm or corporation. Usually, they have relocated from an urban area to the suburbs and feel as though they have "made it." They are non-participatory in the educational or political movements in the town in which they reside. I would describe this group as the "want-to-be population." They believe that they are more successful than they are. The main focus during a social gathering is on which side of town a person lives and the make and model of automobile that is driven.

There is a very different focus of conversation when in the company of the "Black elite." While they are the professionals with whom the first group aspires to be or often thinks that they are, this group has attained wealth in every sense of the term. They live in the most desirable areas of town, sought after by both Blacks and Whites. Spending an evening in their company makes you feel as though you are with the White affluent. During one such event to which I was invited, the guest list included several journalists and television news anchors; high profile surgeons and attorneys; physicians and business consultants to the stars. The conversation was centered on the value of their stocks and investments, their vacation homes, and the Ivy League schools attended by their children. I always attempt to initiate a conversation about racism regardless of which group I am within. The response is the same—there is no interest. My educated peers now view me as an angry Black woman—a militant.

Collectively speaking, educated Black folks have adopted a standard of living that relies on "how much we have and how we can make others believe that we have more." Most threatening is the reality that we are raising our children with the same belief system. Successful Blacks often belittle the parenting styles of their socially and economically deprived counterparts, but the reality is that the method of parenting adopted by the successful Black is not much better. Our children, similar to those from the 'hood' are living their lives as if they are participants in a rap video or reality show. We are making no effort to ensure that they have the tools to survive within a society that is against them.

THE ECONOMY

"The way to lure the Black consumer to Black businesses
is to use White folks as bait."
Attallah Ali—Activist

There once existed a region in our country where Black businesses flourished and Black people felt a sense of self-pride, togetherness, and self-determination. The time was the early 1900's and the place was the Greenwood section of Tulsa, Oklahoma.

The thirty-five square block sector was the only area in Oklahoma where Black people were permitted to live, work, attend school, and shop. It became known as Black Wall Street, and the circulation of the Black dollar generated great wealth for many business owners. There were schools, hospitals, hotels, movie theatres, grocery stores, a library and much more. Then, in 1921, a Black man was accused of raping a White woman, so an angry mob of Whites burned down 1400 buildings and killed dozens.

I don't believe that we could ever recreate such a powerful economic vehicle, as we no longer view our "Blackness" as a factor that can bring us together. We are now so many levels of "Black" that we can't even agree when *we* are being discriminated against. There are so many groups of "Black" that some believe that they are "less" Black as they do not relate to the struggles as African-Americans because they are Jamaican, African, or from some other Black island. Unfortunately, they fail to realize that the color of their skin and the genetic pool from which they come makes them "niggers" to the White establishment, just like the rest of us!

The closest that Black people have come to realizing true self-determination is through the work of the Nation of Islam. Minister Louis Farrakhan has been able to organize and maintain a community of Black people who grow their own food, educate their own children and spend their money within their own community. Interestingly, Farrakhan has always believed in "the centuries-old conspiracy of international Bankers running the world, inciting wars for profit." Sound familiar? (Gates, p.332)

It's 2012 and we Black people have not obtained the economic strength needed to control the destiny of our families and community. We often hear scholars make reference to the pre-civil rights era when we were conscientious about supporting Black business owners. Was it because we understood the importance of self-determination? Or was it because we didn't have a choice? I now believe it was the latter. It seems as though our mission has always been to be accepted and to assimilate within the White establishment rather than to maintain our own independence. As Dr. DeGruy says,

> "We do not control the economy. Others conquer, destroy, and take, we don't. African-Americans have to learn how to think globally and be forward thinking. We don't have a clue about the change that is coming. The world is changing .. . others have grown tired of the U.S. using up resources when others simply want water."

While some don't believe that the effects of slavery are relevant to the plight of Black people, I believe otherwise. The enslavement of Black people by Europeans stripped us of our independence and confidence. We have the misconception that those from other races have a higher intellect, particularly those of Asian descent. The reality is that these people come to the United States with a different value system about family, education, and work. This type of discipline contributes to their educational and economic success.

Comedian Chris Rock addresses the phenomenon in his documentary "Bad Hair" in which he reports that the Koreans have monopolized the Black hair care industry. They will only sell to one another at the wholesale level, locking out Blacks so that they don't have an opportunity to profit from the sale of goods used by their own people. He stated that Black women spend millions of dollars on hair care products, wigs, and hair for weaving and braiding.

Members of the White Slave Masters Union knew that the removal of the shackles from the ankles and wrists provided a physical sense of freedom, but it could not remove the damage from the emotional abuse and degradation that took place over four hundred years. The fetters would forever become a part of the negro mind. This slave mentality would interfere with the re-establishment of self-determination, and we now suffer from "the crabs in the barrel syndrome" which is a feeling of envy that interferes with one's ability to support another for fear that the other will prosper. Is it possible that this is the result of economic slavery, the post-slavery scheme that occurred at the hand of White southerners? Freed slaves would believe that they were sharecroppers of their own farmland, when in fact they would soon find themselves in debt.

They would rent land, buy food on credit and borrow equipment at prices that were inflated, with the understanding that they would pay their debt once they harvested their crops. When they could not fulfill their obligations, they would become property of the penal system. Oftentimes, White citizens could pay off the debt for the sharecropper, and the sharecropper would then work for that person until his debt was paid. Private business owners often rented prisoners who would work for them. This led to an increase in the arrests of Black men for loitering or being drunk in public during harvest time.

Crabs in a Barrel

We now understand that many Black folks suffer from Post Traumatic Slave Disorder. This mentality interferes with our growth and development as a community. Rather than support our own when doing business, we would rather spend money on products sold by other groups. The excuse often used is that "Black folks do not know how to do business. We aren't as professional as others." While this is true in some cases, it is not true in all. There are some Black brothers and sisters who know how to operate a business in a manner that is professional. Our businesses are competitive --- we often have to rely on other groups for support because Black folks are so worried that their contributions to our businesses will move us to the next tax bracket.

As the owner/operator of a preschool for twenty-one years, I have experienced this treatment from my people on a first-hand basis, particularly when my clientele grew to include the children of educated and upper-middle-class Black folks. When the parents would visit my facility, they would oftentimes be disappointed to see that I was Black—particularly the mothers.

In 1991 I began a preschool program in Freehold, New Jersey, for Black and Hispanic boys whose daycare services were terminated by predominately White establishments. These boys would complete successfully my program and move forward to thrive during their formal educational careers. Many of the boys were from socially deprived backgrounds and had been raised by single mothers who were trying to improve their lives. All benefited from the program, as it was based on the premise that "most children are educable when raised in a loving and stimulating environment." Since I believed in the effectiveness of this method, I decided to expand to Teaneck, New Jersey, where I knew that many Black boys were experiencing day care discrimination similar to those in Freehold, even though they were from socio-economic backgrounds that were more stable. Sadly, the response from my more educated counterparts was not as positive. There was an Obstacle --- "Crabs in a Barrel Syndrome."

My first experience occurred when I located a building to purchase. I realized that I was in need of funding for start-up costs. A friend informed me that a classmate with whom we attended high school was the CEO of a Black family-owned mortgage company. While I was not expecting preferential treatment, I expected to have the same opportunity to apply for a loan as any other entrepreneur would. This was not the case. Not only was I not considered for financial assistance, my application was never reviewed. It would be three White men, my current landlords, who would provide me the capital for start-up costs. They were impressed with my mission and my history as a successful businesswoman. During this time, a young Jewish businessman attempted to convince me to open several more preschools in an Orthodox Jewish neighborhood in the Bronx in which he would invest. I did not accept because I wanted to help my people.

Prior to opening, I relied on the patronage and support of childhood friends who vowed to enroll their children in my program or to assist in drumming up business. As early as the open house, I found there to be no support. Even Black couples with whom I was unfamiliar were not impressed that I was a sister even though my resume boasted fifteen years of success in another town and references from an Assistant Prosecutor, several professors, and a host of child care advocates from the town in which my business operated. While my first family to enroll was Black (Mr. & Mrs. Wilson) it was not my Black brethren who would support me, but rather members of the Orthodox Jewish community.

After struggling to keep my doors open for the first eighteen months, my fortunes changed with the enrollment of a young Jewish couple who felt that their toddler could benefit from my program. Once they enrolled, they advised others in their community to enroll their children. They were not concerned that I was Black and Muslim with several other Muslim teachers. They entrusted their children in my care as they appreciated and respected me as a scholar and expert in the area of early childhood development. Members of my own community began to show interest in my services once the Jewish families validated me.

The reality is that we as Black folks would rather utilize our energy to keep a brother or sister down rather than pool our resources to endorse Black business and thwart those companies that expect our "Black dollar, but do not respect it."

The Boycott

As consumers, we must understand the economic infrastructure of this country. The United States of America is a capitalistic society that thrives on the privatization of business. The economy is what drives this beast. Without it, there would be nothing. Sadly, we don't seem to understand this reality, as we do not utilize our economic power to battle issues of racism and discrimination towards our community. Other groups, however, have mastered this approach successfully and use it to their advantage. For example, when OJ Simpson was to make a guest appearance on a major news network to discuss his book, White folks banded together and threatened to boycott the station, the advertisers and anyone else who supported Simpson. The end result was no appearance by Simpson and a public apology by the CEO of the station denouncing the reporter who was going to conduct the interview. This is called "leverage," a bargaining tool that Black folks do not understand how to implement—for several reasons.

First, *we* are not cognizant of our economic power, but the establishment is. They know that Black folks, particularly women, spend the most money on soft goods (clothing, shoes, and handbags), hair supplies, beauty products and luxury items.

Secondly, the boycott which can be extremely effective is not an option because we don't understand our economic strength. No company wants to lose business because of mistreatment or accusations of racial discrimination. It's clear that many Black people do not want to participate in protests or demonstrations for fear of losing their jobs, which is why the boycott is a perfect way to participate with full anonymity. Black people should shut down the commercial segment of Christmas to flex their economic power. This tool could be utilized to demand that the problem of police brutality within our major cities be addressed. Imagine what would happen if Black folks around the nation only shopped for the bare necessities during the months of November and December and did not purchase luxury items or gifts for the holidays.

Finally, and most damaging, is the reality that we will not react without approval from a leading Black selected by the media to call a plan of action. That approach is no longer practical for the style of racism that affects the Black community today. We must stop waiting for another Malcolm or Martin. We must teach our young people to become the two. The leading Blacks use the masses for their own benefit. They are not speaking for the Black community, but we continue to allow them to pretend to do so. Such leading Blacks call for action but then fail to follow through as they settle our battle at the bargaining table—without us.

The end result is that we in the Black community have no real bargaining power because we continuously make the same mistake and do not follow through with our threat. We are passive and easily distracted.

The Letter Writing Campaign

It must be understood that while there is power in numbers, there is also individual strength. A consumer, when dissatisfied with a product or the service in a specific establishment, should contact the public relations department. You would be surprised with the response. As mentioned earlier, no company wants to have a customer who is unhappy as one unhappy customer could represent many. If you are complaining, their thought is that there are others who feel the same. They would rather address a problem then to allow it to erupt into an out-of-control situation that may interfere with their cash flow.

Reporting the Disrespectful Salesperson

Learn to move through the store with entitlement, just as White folks do. Do not accept being followed while shopping or having a salesperson mistreat you. Exercise your right to complain when displeased. When feeling a sense of mistreatment, never argue with the cashier or salesperson. Ask to speak to the manager. Doing so will set a "zero tolerance for racism" precedent. Don't second-guess yourself. Chances are, if you feel as though you are being discriminated against, you probably are. We must no longer be concerned with what people think if we call the race card. Imagine what would happen if we all accepted this rule for shopping. It would change the way that Black shoppers are viewed.

Demand Respect While Shopping

Over the last two decades we have experienced an influx of small businesses operated by Korean, Vietnamese, and Indian merchants in the Black community. These business owners have adopted the stereotypical beliefs about Black people and treat us accordingly as we spend OUR money within their establishments.

We fail to understand the power of our Black dollar. We should each demand to be greeted upon entering and thanked as we leave. I have lost count of the many incidents in which we (BWARE) have had to advocate for a brother or sister wrongfully treated while shopping. I firmly remind the shop owner that if we "Black folks" stopped shopping in their store, they would have to close their doors.

In 2006, members of BWARE organized a boycott against a Dollar Store in Elmwood Park, New Jersey, owned and operated by an Indian family. The salespeople were extremely rude and disrespectful to their Black customers. The women organized a demonstration for four hours in front of the store on a Saturday afternoon. Close to one hundred shoppers supported the protest and took their business elsewhere. To date, the owners of the store are more respectful to their Black customers.

Support Five Black Establishments

Make an extra effort to support at least five businesses that are Black owned and encourage friends and family members to do the same. This could include your physician, day care provider, accountant, plumber or hairdresser. You will have to do your homework and hire those whom you feel meet your standards of professionalism. But just as you expect the best quality of service, the Black owner expects the same.

I must admit that during my twenty-one years in business as an educator and nursery school owner, my most difficult clients have been Black folks—not the socially deprived single mothers to whom I provided service to in the early 90's, but the "all American Black power couples" who disrespected my rules and regulation as a business owner. They challenged my every request and expressed feelings of disbelief when I reminded them of payment due or when I exercised my authority. I found that other Black business owners had similar experiences. We concluded that such behavior is descriptive of Post Traumatic Slave Disorder, as such conduct while doing business in a White establishment would not occur.

The Black Business Owner

If you are a new business owner, strive for perfection. Learn to be savvy when first opening. Do not focus on the financial gain, but rather growing your customer/clientele base. Learn to crawl before you walk. The most effective approach is to under-sell your competitors, offer more for less and train your staff to be professional at all times. You could employ one or more of these approaches:

- If you operate a hair salon, **always** open on time and demand that your stylists arrive promptly as well. Ensure that your establishment is always clean and orderly. Play music that is not offensive to clients and offer beverages, fruit and other snacks as a way to show your appreciation to your clients. Require each stylist to maintain all information shared with him/her from clients as confidential.
- As a freelance carpenter or contractor, don't attempt to make millions from one customer. Be reasonably priced, honest, and most of all, reliable. Learn your craft before offering services. Always be professional.
- When operating a clothing or shoe store, **always** open on time. The most common complaint is that Black people are never on time. Train staff to be pleasant and to speak to customers as they arrive. Undersell the competitor or sell at a price that is competitive. **Never** overprice merchandise.

As a seasoned business owner follow the same approaches for success as the new owner. Always be professional, punctual, and hire those who best reflect the image you want to portray.

Save a Percentage of Your Salary

While this may be a difficult time to save, attempt to put something away, no matter how small. Choose an amount that you can commit to on a weekly, biweekly, or monthly schedule. Remember that change adds up. When you break a bill put the coins in a jar for one year or so. This can be used for birthday gifts or for the holidays. Start teaching your children the value of money while they are still young so that they develop good spending habits as they grow into young adults.

The Recession

During an interview on *Like It Is*, Gil Noble discussed with Dr. Joy DeGruy, clinical psychologist, how "Black people can expect to move through these economic times." She began with a focus on health and stress. Dr. DeGruy proposed that Black people must focus on good health and reducing stress. She stated that traditional education does not address the needs of African-Americans. Traditional stressors that are associated with Caucasian people are those stressors described as "ordinary." Those stressors inflicted as the result of racism are not addressed, leaving African-American people no mechanisms for coping with "racism" which is the number one cause of stress in our lives.

Dr. DeGruy goes on to advise that Black people must pay attention to the behavior of White people to determine our destiny in the USA. She revisited the tragedy of a man who burned down his house then flew his plane into a building occupied by a division of the Internal Revenue Service because he felt that they were unfair in their requests of him as a taxpayer. Dr. DeGruy goes on to suggest that if this man has the means to own a home and a plane was feeling so overwhelmed that he initiated such violence, what does that mean for African-American's during such difficult economic times? She asserts that "when White people have a cold, we have pneumonia."

It's imperative that we learn how to function in a capitalistic society—one which claims "free enterprise." We must teach our children that they too can control where they spend their money. We should discuss with them the importance of saving and investing. Parents can simply encourage children to save a percentage of their allowance or monetary gifts received for birthdays or holidays. Older children should understand the importance of the "credit report score," as credit scores will determine their access to low interest rate loans.

The final goal should be to re-create a Black community that is self-determined and able to function without the assistance from others. There is no reason why every major city in this country should not have a neighborhood of thriving Black businesses, including schools, recreation centers, banks, restaurants and other establishments.

Finally, we small business owners must develop a stronger sense of professionalism and solid work ethic to lure back the Black consumer. We cannot expect to have patrons support our establishment if we are unreliable and not well prepared in our area of specialty.

TROUBLE WITH OUR YOUTH

"I don't be in the project hallway talkin' bout how I
be in the projects all day."
Jay Z.—Lyricist, Rapper

As a teenager growing up in the suburbs of New York in the 1980's, I never thought that I would become an advocate for those with whom I had nothing in common. My childhood was typical in a suburban sense. I was raised in a town that was the first in the country to integrate its school system voluntarily and was well-known for the diverse population of residents. My parents relocated from Brooklyn to provide a better quality of life for my older sister and me. Both of my parents were college graduates, and maintained a strong sense of "community and work ethic." They were employed as city workers with the State of New York. My father always had a second job and still managed to work as a tennis instructor during his free time. While our household was somewhat dysfunctional, my parents set the foundation for my work as an activist and business owner.

My mother was raised in Freehold, New Jersey sixty miles south of New York City and one of the last towns in the country to integrate its school system. During the 1940's and 1950's her family operated a grocery store out of their home and helped to feed those neighbors who were less fortunate. To date, my mother at eighty-three-years of age serves on several community boards and is an active member of Habitat for Humanity.

My father, raised in Harlem, was a mentor to young Black boys from the city. He and several other brothers organized a tennis program that would keep these young and vulnerable boys off the streets. Many came from homes without fathers and with mothers who were on drugs or were overwhelmed with work and a number of other children. My father and his partners acted as surrogate fathers to these boys, as they would attend school meetings with their mothers or guardians and act as advocates when any of the boys experienced legal problems.

Nevertheless, while it is clear that my experiences as a child would impact who I would become, it was not until early adulthood that I would experience the true racism that would eventually change my life.

Saving Black boys

The year was 1990 and I decided to leave my job in retail management and explore a career in early childhood education. I was hired as a teacher in a predominantly White preschool in Freehold. During my time there, I observed the White teachers as they handled our Black babies, particularly the boys. On one occasion a young White teacher did not want to brush the sand out of a two-year-old Black boy's hair because she did not like the way his hair felt. On another occasion, I listened as two older White teachers described an eighteen-month-old Black baby as a "monkey." When I brought my concerns to the attention of the Asian director, I was told that the teachers loved the children and did not have intentions that were malicious. I considered informing the parents, but I refrained from doing so, since the parents were so proud that their little Black boys had been accepted into the program that they would bypass me each day to greet the White teachers.

This experience resulted in my opening a preschool that became populated by Black boys who were dismissed from larger White centers due to behavior that was described as socially inappropriate. Most of these boys would move through my program and begin their formal education with great success.

It was from that point that I realized that our children needed support—that we should not look to others to raise and manage our legacy. Sadly, I have observed a decrease in the involvement of African-American adults within the lives of their children.

Police Brutality

One spring day in Harlem, a Black man was murdered by a White police officer. There was a rally called by a popular civil rights activist. The leaflet that circulated through the streets read as followed:

ONE MORE NEGRO BRUTALLY BEATEN AND
KILLED! SHOT DOWN LIKE A DOG BY THE POLICE.
ALL OUT HARLEM . . .

The year was 1942, the man killed was Wallace Armstrong, and the activist was Adam Clayton Powell. Other than the word "negro" one would believe that this is a flyer prepared after the murder of Sean Bell in 2006.

Rev. Powell called for a mass meeting of members from the Black community. He urged an immediate investigation of the police department. How is it that we are still demanding the same action against the NYPD as was requested over sixty years ago? Have we not made any progress? Apparently, we haven't. The one factor that has changed since 1942 is that there is an increase in the brutalization of Black girls and women at the hands of the police in our country. This form of hatred is the result of racism that has been institutionalized and not addressed by the Black community. We have not been effective in the infiltration of such mistreatment.

During the summer of 2007, a young activist, Katrina Phillips, from Yonkers, New York, addressed the increase of police brutality in her community. Ms. Phillips, a member of National Action Network at the time, organized a rally to which she invited Al Sharpton to deliver a message to the youth. As we stood among several hundred teens and young adults, Sharpton's caravan raced across the field as if he were the President of the United States. As he stepped out of his SUV, the crowd cheered, clapped and chanted his name. He stepped onto the stage and stated, "If you love yourself, you won't get shot." "Wonderful!" I thought to myself. "This man has hundreds of teens and young adults at his attention and this is his message? What about those who do love themselves and behave in a manner that is considered acceptable socially? Are they safe against being brutalized or murdered by the police? I think not."

The suburbs of New York City are not immune to such brutality at the hands of the "men in blue." During the fall of September 2007, in Teaneck New Jersey, a group of eleven-year-old children were walking home from school down the same tree lined street that I walked down in the 70's. The back door of the school leads out onto a dead end street that continues to a main road. Several hundred children walk this path on their way home from school. Many of them walk in the street, as there is not enough space for them to walk together on the sidewalk. Over time, the neighbors began to complain that each day at 3:00 pm the students would fill the entire street making it impossible for residents to drive in and out of the block. On one particular day, police were sent to ensure that the students remained on the sidewalk. When several filtered into the streets, rather than informing the students that they were expected to remain closer to the sidewalk for their own safety, the officers became physical throwing several children into the police car denying them access to their cell phones to call their parents. One girl resisted and was wrestled to the ground by a male officer, then handcuffed and thrown into the back of the police car. He then drove them back where they were given tickets for jaywalking.

A week later, there was a town hall meeting for the parents, the students, and those who lived on the street where the problems had occurred. Upon arrival, several members from BWARE were approached by two Black women who announced, "This is not about race. These Black children here are very disrespectful. They deserved to be given a summons." We replied, "It *is* about race." We went on to say that *our* Black children do know how to behave and the implication that they do not suggests that they are inferior genetically.

The meeting was facilitated by the Black male principal, who was clearly used as the scapegoat but was too ignorant to realize that fact. He spoke in favor of the police and explained how it was he who had requested the presence of the police. We questioned, "As a Black man, did you not feel any connection to these children as you retreated to the use of the police rather than addressing the problem yourself?"

White residents described the drive down their street as aggravating, as they had to navigate between hundreds of children. One man went on to say that he was afraid that they would get hurt. A Black woman responded, "What did you think that you would get when you purchased your home several feet away from a junior high school?" An Asian women stood up in support of her neighbors and said, "One day two boys were running and laughing, chasing each other." A person in the audience asked, "Were they on your property and disturbing the property of others?" She responded, "No, but they were loud." This is a perfect example of the double standard rule. White kids can be drunk and loud in public, and when they are, they are simply having fun. This is not so for Black children. Whites and those who attempt to assimilate with Whites feel threatened by Black children, regardless of their behavior and particularly in large groups.

This heated discussion continued for over two hours, heated at times, as **some** of the Black parents were clearly upset by the events that had taken place. One man shared with the audience his concern that his eleven-year-old would now have a misdemeanor on his record. The Chief of Police reassured him that it was simply a misdemeanor and that it did not hold much weight. Immediately, members of BWARE asked the Chief, "How would you feel if your little White eleven-year-old-son had a misdemeanor?" He responded by stating that this was not about race. Once again, we responded, "It indeed was about race." Why should we as Black parents be comfortable with the fact that our children have an illegal offense that could follow them for the rest of their lives? Furthermore, why should a ride in the back of a police car be a normal occurrence for our children? The Black woman seated behind us stated that she hoped there would be no lawsuits against the town because that would result in a tax increase. I couldn't believe what I was hearing. This person was more concerned with the possible increase in her taxes than about whether justice would prevail for her own child.

There were some members in the audience who focused on the practice of jaywalking by members of the Orthodox Jewish community on the other side of town on the night of their Sabbath. The presence of police in their community was to assist, not to arrest.

This was a clear case of racism. While there were some members of the audience as upset as we, others (Blacks) were accepting and forgiving. Sadly, it was the testimony of the children involved that put the reality of this crime into perspective. One little eleven-year-old girl, who looked to be eight instead, explained in a soft-spoken voice how she felt violated and mistreated when approached by the police. A boy, who too looked much younger than eleven, explained how he was not even permitted to call his parents. Hearing the voices of these children broke my heart. These were not the rough thugs about which the Black woman spoke earlier. These were innocent little children whose backpacks were probably bigger than they were.

The next day we contacted several of the parents whose children were involved and asked them whether they would be interested in filing a lawsuit against the township. One woman, an attorney, said that she could not because she worked for the firm that represented the school. The family of the girl who was physically assaulted wanted to forget the problem (there was talk that they were not in the country legally and were afraid of deportation). The last family did not feel as though they would be effective without the other families. Our last attempt was to have the tickets dropped so that these children did not have to appear in front of the judge. We were unsuccessful.

How could either of those concerns be more important than fighting for the rights of our children? What was wrong with us? How would the Jewish community respond if their children were targeted and harassed by police as they walked to Synagogue? Would they offer such excuses? I think not.

That afternoon, I sat outside another junior high school in town (also populated by Black students) to observe the behavior of the police officer as he acted as crossing guard. He was an overweight White officer with a big red face and red neck. He rudely directed the children to cross the street in a superior tone, barely looking at them. They simply looked at him and continued walking.

In New York City, activists Agnes Johnson and her daughter Mia Cruz monitored the actions of New York City police officers as they harassed young children going to and from school. On several occasions, they harassed Black students as they walked through the street on which their school was located. Many having to travel outside of their communities would have to walk through predominately White communities. They would be reminded by the police that they needed to "keep it moving" as they did not belong in the area. This illegal practice eventually led to a physical altercation in which a student was injured by the police. The student was taken in the patrol car to the precinct. Sisters Johnson and Cruz arrived moments later as witnesses for the student. Upon his release the activists assisted him in filing a report with internal affairs.

In November 2010, public reports stated that a Hispanic police officer from the Bronx admitted that his superiors expected he and other officers to write tickets and make arrests whether someone was in violation or not in order to meet monthly quotas. They were expected to target people of color, particularly those coming to and from school. One incident as remembered by the officer was a case where two school-aged boys were chasing each other. After one fell down, both were issued tickets and arrested for unlawful assembly. The boys were taken to headquarters where the charges were eventually dropped, but the officer still received points for the summons.

When Our Children Need Help

The problem with Black boys is that they grow up to be Black men and it's safe to say that Black men have had to fight for a place in this country since having been brought to the United States like chained animals. Dr. Anderson Franklin describes this invisibility as an inner struggle with feeling that one's talents, abilities, personality and worth are not valued or recognized because of prejudice and racism (p. 4).

We must focus not only on the brutal and illegal behavior as exhibited by the police on the streets but also on their reaction to Black children when they are in crisis. One such incident was described by a middle-aged couple who had recently learned that their three-year-old child was named as one of several children who was physically and verbally abused by his previous day care provider. The abuse began when the child was ten-months-old and ended when he was three-years of age. The parents were not surprised about the accusations, as they had removed their son from the day care program several months earlier because of their own suspicions. As a toddler, he would scream when getting his diaper changed. He did not develop age appropriate language skills and as a preschooler he would resort to frequent unexplained tantrums and episodes of crying. According to the parents, when they were contacted by the County Department of Child Abuse in New Jersey, it was requested that they allow the child to meet with authorities. The parents agreed immediately even though his ability to communicate was limited.

Upon arriving at the precinct, their three-year-old was not greeted by a soft-spoken professional, but rather by an insensitive White male detective, who approached the little boy and his parents with "we need him to come with us." His mother and father, perplexed by the unprofessionalism of those who they believed cared about the well-being of their son, asked whether they would be able to observe the process as their son was in an unfamiliar place. The detective repeated his initial demand that they wait in the waiting area as failure to do so would interfere with the investigation. They watched in horror as their three-year-old son was taken down a long corridor through three locked doors. Moments later, the boy's father demanded that their son be brought back to them. He and his wife both felt as though their child was not treated with care and respect. Their decision to end the investigative process with their son resulted in a chaotic situation with the detectives and police involved in the matter. The team of officers continuously reminded the parents that they ruined the case by not allowing their son to complete the interview. This information was confusing as there were a group of other children, many of them older, who could have provided information that would have been more helpful.

During this time, a Black woman who was in the company of the police when the family arrived at the precinct, introduced herself as "a social worker from Department of Youth and Family Services" and informed the parents that they should allow their son to stay with the detectives. The mother asked, "Why did you not introduce yourself sooner?" She was hurt that this Black woman from an agency organized to protect children did not feel the need advocate for her baby boy as White detectives treated him like a teenage convict rather than a three-year-old victim of abuse.

The family would later learn that the case against the former babysitter was dismissed, as there was not enough evidence. As a Black woman, she would have been prosecuted if the victims were White, since the lives of White children have more value than that of their Black counterparts.

This mistreatment in the form of psychological abuse towards young Black babies occurs more often than we think. Our children are viewed as less than human by the "boys in blue" even when they are most vulnerable. There was no concern for the psychological well-being of the little children who were taken away from their parents when they needed their support the most. The act of separating child and parent can be compared to the act of removing the child from his or her family during the sale of African-Americans during slavery.

The War on Drugs

In February 2012 Senator Golden from New York initiated a campaign against illegal drug use at the hands of young teenagers from Staten Island, where the rate of overdosing is the highest in the country. Mr. Senator expressed his concerns that this particular suburban area continues to struggle with the abuse of "Oxycotin" by its teenage residents. He mentions during an interview that "these teens are from prominent families and good homes—not the typical drug using kid." He goes on to inform the public that "we must save our children." One could guess that "our children" mean "White children."

A society that operates on a capitalistic ideology will do anything to ensure its growth, even at the expense of its citizens. Since the White establishment has never embraced Black people, who best to target in a conspiracy of illicit drugs and violence but the most vulnerable—*poor* Black people. According to Gary Webb (1999) there is no doubt that the government wants to import cocaine into the neighborhoods of poor Black people.

Black men have been the scapegoats for the drug epidemic in this country for decades. This conspiracy by the government would eventually engulf generations of young Black men and boys who would choose drug dealing over a low paying job or school, oftentimes resulting in death or prison time. Their vulnerability and desire for money and material items would weaken them. To date we have not educated our boys on the history of the drug trade in the United States of America and the role that they have been selected to play. I'm sure that exposure to this information would have saved many from a life on the streets.

Illegal drugs and capitalism are a lethal combination. As we know, capitalism focuses on the privatization of businesses. Film director Kevin Booth provided an in depth look at drugs in America in his documentary *American Drugs: the Last White Hope*. Booth began with the official campaign against drugs in 1971 when President Richard Nixon called for "a war on drugs." By 1973, the Drug Enforcement Agency (DEA) was organized. The government would lead the country to believe that they were fighting to decrease the use and sale of illicit drugs while they were in fact filtering hard drugs into poor Black neighborhoods and incarcerating those who would use them, rather than focusing their efforts on the large companies that laundered drug money like the banks.

According to Booth, there are over one million non-violent drug offenders in jails across the nation. This would be the result of the national drug schedule which has a rating from one to five—one most dangerous and five the least. Marijuana would be registered as number one, designated as more dangerous than cocaine and heroin. It's described as a gateway drug that leads to the use of those drugs that are more potent. How could marijuana be more accessible and more likely to lead to drug use than alcohol? It seems that marijuana was registered as a schedule one drug as a way to criminalize Black men. According to Booth, the only reason the drug prohibition for cocaine (known as the White man's drug) was enforced in the 1980's was to protect White women from Black males.

Booth describes the "war on drugs" as the largest and most expensive war in the country. There are more drugs today than ten years ago—leading some of us to believe that the "war on drugs" is used as a diversion so the sale of drugs can continue to feed the machine that feeds the private companies.

In the 1980's laws were passed to allow prisons to be privatized. A prison's survival relies on its cells being occupied by low-level drug offenders, which is why many laws were created to impose harsher penalties on those caught with drugs most likely used by Blacks.

Gary Webb, author of *Dark Alliance* describes how the Central Intelligence Agency was the government's source of information and how the Director of Operations has been the main culprit behind agency scandals as relating to "the war on drugs."

In the early 1980's, Ricky Ross, also known as "Freeway Ricky Ross" operated a crack empire in South Central Los Angeles, as his connection to a Columbian drug dealer provided him with the cocaine used to make to crack. According to Webb, members of the CIA were involved with the drug trafficking of cocaine into the country. Filmmaker Kevin Booth recalls the same public service message against "crack cocaine" in the 1980's that aired simultaneously on every major network. The announcement, while informing the public about the harm of "crack" described the effects and even the cheap cost to purchase—almost like an orchestrated advertisement campaign.

In 1986, it was learned that Oliver North, National Security Council Staff Member under Ronald Reagan, was accused of selling weapons to Iran while drugs were permitted to be flown to America. Reports reveal that the government sent agents to marketing school to learn how to market drugs. They imported cocaine and relied on Ross to turn it into crack and sell it. Manuel Noriega (Panama) was told by CIA agents that he could have free run on drugs in the US if America could run weapons into Nicaragua. Some officials believe that Ross did not invest enough money at the local level to bribe local authorities to allow him to continue to sell drugs, which is why he was eventually arrested. (Booth 2011)

During Bill Clinton's term as President, he became "the Black people's President." Typically, we as Black folks embrace any politician from whom we receive attention. In Clinton's case it was his debut on the saxophone that gained his acceptance within the Black community. Clinton, like earlier Presidents didn't care at all about our community. According to Webb, he organized a drug agency led by Barry McCaffrey that focused on expanding and filling the prisons rather than fighting the "war on drugs." Seventeen billion dollars was budgeted for the "war on drugs." The funds were spent to keep drugs on our streets and our boys and men in jail. Millions of nonviolent pot smokers were arrested under McCaffrey's term. Clinton played sympathetic politician while McCaffrey did the dirty work.

In Tulia, Texas, a police sweep of the Black community sought to find drugs and users within that area. Those found in possession of drugs were given 99-375 years in sentences that came to be described as "ethnic cleansing." In fact, this sweep by redneck police was an attempt to garner grant money for the town. Ultimately, in 2004, victims of Tulia were awarded 5 million dollars in a wrongful conviction.

According to the documentary, *The American Drug War—Last White Hope*, the "drug machine" has stimulated the economy in the United States for decades. The commentator goes on to say that we, the citizens, have been misled into believing that our government has been diligently working to overcome this problem with their "war on drugs campaign" when in fact the campaign was a decoy to divert the attention from the public to the government's involvement in the sale and distribution of drugs in this country.

Illicit drugs have devastated the Black community, with addiction and incarceration running at high rates among men and women who were drug abuses, involved in drug trafficking or gang violence. Why would the White establishment choose Black life over guaranteed income? Many private businesses were benefitting from this activity, including, but not limited to, the mortgage companies. People had become so addicted that they stopped paying their mortgages and subsequently walked away from their homes. The mortgage companies then purchased the foreclosed properties and resold them at a higher rate.

It's imperative that we understand the role of propaganda in the hands of the media. The American media has reported that the Taliban in Afghanistan is responsible for the rise in heroin, as the group controls the poppy fields in their country. However, according to *The American War on Drugs* the CIA has allowed and supported the production of opium. When Afghanistan was controlled by the Taliban, the sale of opium was down. Once the USA took over, heroin production was on the rise. One of the many conspiracy theories is that Bin Laden blew up the twin towers because Bush made money off the opium in his country and then cut Bin Laden out of the profits—all in the name of Capitalism.

Gang Violence

It's rare that one is told the history of gang violence in the United States. When we think of those who partake in such activity, we think immediately of men and women of color as this is portrayed on television. According to the documentary *American Gangs* the Irish, Jews, and Italians started gang violence in New York City. By the 1850's, politicians began using gangs to further their campaigns for election to office by investing their interest in the groups as a voting bloc. This information must be conveyed to Blacks so that they understand that gang violence is not the way of our culture.

Studies have shown that the current gang problem in our country is caused by young Black and brown men and women, who, in most situations, have not finished high school and have lost their way in the world with no one to provide them direction. The spread of gang culture from one state to another is the direct result of the crack epidemic in South Central Los Angeles. According to *The War on Drugs*, gang members buy crack cheaply in L.A. and then sell it at inflated rates in other parts of the country. The Black community has lost a generation of young men and women to a life style that is a direct result of the influx of illicit drugs. It's impossible to resolve the problem until we address from where the problem has come; but why would our government be interested in winning the war on drugs?

Through experience as an educator and community activist, I have learned from my peers that there is little empathy for those children involved in gang crime and violence. Many feel that these young people have options, as there have been many before them raised under the same social conditions who have chosen to become productive citizens. It is disheartening to know that those who have realized both educational and economic success cannot feel a sense of empathy or sadness towards our children who have lost their way. We, as educated Black folks, are obligated to guide and assist those who may be deprived due to their social and economic situation. While it is clear that all cannot be helped, there are those men and women who simply need a mentor or someone to provide them with encouragement.

The Village

Historically speaking, it *was* the village that raised the Black child. Pre-Civil Rights era, Black parents had no concerns as to who would ensure that their children behaved well while not in their care. It was understood that the teacher, extended family members, or even neighbors could discipline and/or spank when a child misbehaved. Such an approach to childrearing was effective and encouraged appropriate behavior when a child was away from home, as "the village" was not isolated to one particular street, but rather stretched across town. The key to its success was that there was someone who knew a member of the child's family and would report disrespect or unacceptable behavior or in some instances, administer a spanking that would be the prelude to the butt whipping that was to come upon the child's arrival at home.

Unfortunately, this village mentality no longer exists. The "all about me" approach to living that we have adopted from the White establishment has become the way in which we now live our lives. This has interfered with the way that we raise our children. We are often offended when another adult reports the misbehavior of our children, fearing that the focus is on our parenting rather than a more genuine concern. As a result, our children are aware of this, thus minimizing their fear of neighbors or other members of their communities. I would be more than gracious if another adult informed me that my children were not behaving appropriately, no matter how minor the behavior as they would be aware that someone is always watching.

On one occasion, a 'sister' who happens to be a teacher in the community in which I work, reported to me that *our* children were downstairs in the parking lot behaving in a manner that was embarrassing. She went on to say that there were a group of high school students (girls and boys) cursing and play fighting as members from the Jewish community watched in disgust as they walked past. I asked her if she made an effort to talk to them. She replied, "Oh please. These kids today will curse you out." In complete disagreement, I went downstairs, only to witness about twenty-five teenagers yelling and chasing one another. As I approached, some of the girls, hands on hips, looked at me as if to say "what does this____want?" I introduced myself and went on to say that I was a business owner and community activist. I informed them that *I* understood that they were simply having fun as most teenagers, but as Black children, their behavior appeared threatening to others. I told them that White folks and some Blacks have very low expectations of them and that they should not give them reasons to validate that belief. I explained to them that the other business owners (all Asian) would call the police if they did not discontinue their wild behavior. Finally, I told them that they are welcome to ring my bell if ever harassed by the police or anyone else *only* if they were behaving well at the time. Not surprisingly, these teenagers were grateful and responded to my suggestions.

I do not believe that our children are genetically inferior to other children. Believing that they do not know how to behave or how to be respectful is unfair. It is the way in which we approach them. The way that the 'sister' spoke to me about the teenagers is how she would have approached the situation.

Parenting

We as Black people have chosen to raise our children according to the approach to parenting utilized by the dominate culture. Black parents do not understand that there are two different Americas, one for White children and the other for their Black counterparts. White children don't have to accept rules and boundaries because as they grow, these children will not be held to the same standards of "perfection" as Black children will be. This choice of parenting is not limited to that of the underclass, as mentioned by Bill Cosby during his speech on July 7, 2004 at a fundraiser for the National Association of the Advancement of Colored People (NAACP). While the socially and economically deprived may not be cognizant of the need to discipline properly, in most cases they do try, unlike we educated Black folk who have chosen to over-indulge our children with no boundaries. We give unconditionally, thus creating a generation of spoiled children with a disregard for rules and regulations. If I remember correctly, Mr. Cosby had some difficulty with his own children.

Through both personal and professional experience, I have witnessed members of my peer group allow their preschool age children to be disrespectful to them and to other figures of authority. These parents have chosen to allow their young children to be the decision makers in the household. Reasoning, bargaining, and choices replace the more effective approaches to parenting in which the parents set the tone. The children are encouraged to question those adults (including teachers) who may request the completion of a specific task. This behavior is encouraged without appropriate intervention until the parents can no longer tolerate the embarrassing episodes when out in public or when in the company of others. It is at this point that parents expect to undo four or five years of submissive parenting. Their choice to permit such poor behavior creates a situation that affects their children in social situations with teachers, peers and others.

As first-time parents, my husband and I chose the wrong approach to parenting for our strong-willed Black boy. We felt as though we had to mold a "mini adult" who would command attention when he entered a room and verbalize every thought and challenge each request. We explained every event and situation in which he was present, whether it involved him or not. This continued until my son was two-and-a-half or so, when I realized that his behavior was not cute but rather annoying. Our toddler believed that he was privileged to participate in every conversation in which we were involved. He did not understand his boundaries. I realized that my job as a mother was to prepare my son to be in the company of other people, including but not limited to teachers, relatives, friends and, one day, a wife. His need to be the center of attention, no matter when and where he was became embarrassing. It was clear that we were creating a monster and needed to implement an approach to parenting that would allow him to realize his fullest potential. In doing so, there were strict guidelines and boundaries that he was required to respect. Failure to do so resulted in the removal of toys or privileges.

This battle has continued over the last ten years and did not improve until my husband and I separated (with no intentions of minimizing the importance of a father figure). He and I had different approaches to parenting that interfered with the way in which we raised our children. I am a disciplinarian and believe in rules, whereas he does not. Children respect boundaries and respond well when they are implemented appropriately. Having worked with behaviorally challenged children, I have been able to control the most difficult child in a structured learning environment that is entrenched in consistent rules and regulations. Children know what is expected of them and respond accordingly. I now practice the same advice that I offer to other parents. My children understand that their personal property is earned due to good behavior—if their behavior is unacceptable, privileges are removed.

In the early 90's when I opened my first preschool, I remember meeting with the parents of a little Black boy whose behavior was unacceptable and disrespectful. His poor behavior interfered with his ability to thrive. He was the nephew of one of the most recognized celebrities in the nation. His mother was a successful attorney and his father an engineer. They lived in the more affluent part of town and drove luxury vehicles. During our meeting, I expressed my concerns regarding this child's behavior. The father informed me that they were raising him similar to the way in which his Jewish co-workers were raising their children. In disbelief, I explained that their son is not Jewish and that they were doing him a disservice. I reminded him of the child's aggressive and uncontrolled behavior when either of them arrived to take him home at the end of the day. The father went on to say that they did not want to break his spirit.

Eventually, the child was removed from my program and enrolled in an affluent, predominately White day school. According to a reliable source, the child's behavior caused him great difficulty in school. A year later the family moved out of state.

Black children cannot be raised in the same manner in which White children or those of other races are raised. My children and I often frequent a public library in a town populated by Koreans. During our visits, the children are often loud, rude, and out of control. They spent their time jumping and standing on furniture, wrestling and knocking over books as their mothers look on. Occasionally, the librarian would come over and explain that the library is a quiet place. As I watched each performance in disbelief, I reminded my children that if those children were little Black boys and girls, the Police would arrive with stun guns and pepper spray.

We have been raised to believe that "other" children, i.e., Asians, are much smarter and better behaved. These myths have damaged our development of self-confidence. One relative mentioned to my daughter that since her school is predominately Korean, the children must be well-behaved. She went on to say "Their parents are extremely strict." From where would she get such information? Parents of Asian cultures often value education, and this means that they usually teach good study habits and support education, as for discipline, it seems to be non-existing.

Our children must be prepared to function in a White racist society. While I believe in "Black schools" as long as they are equipped with the appropriate resources so that the children can compete with their White counterparts, I do not believe that all Black teachers are capable of providing such a service. My experience as a parent and educator is that there are Black teachers who suffer from Post Traumatic Slave Disorder as coined by Dr. Joy Degruy. Their influences can be more damaging than that of the ignorant White teacher.

We must focus on how best to serve our children. Failure to do so will result in the loss of a generation and the future of our children. Let's treat them like our most valuable resource.

Discipline

Gone are the days of old fashioned punishment. We are so busy over-indulging our children that we have lost sight of the true meaning of parenting. We no longer set boundaries nor do we guide our children in a way that will be supportive of their social and personal development. This is a problem in both single and dual parent households thus resulting in more Black children exhibiting public behavior that is unacceptable socially.

As a disciplinarian, I expect my children to perform to the best of their abilities in school and to behave in a manner that is acceptable socially. If they fail, there are consequences. For example:

- My oldest son has always given me a run for my money, even as a preschooler. He was not permitted to attend several birthday parties and also missed one or two of his own for poor behavior. As he got a bit older, I would require him to write "I will do a better job in school" on every line in a 150-page spiral notebook.

- He eventually grew into the school jock and ladies' man, all at the age of twelve. This attention became overwhelming for this little charmer, and he began to be somewhat disrespectful to the teachers and to slack off in his schoolwork. Immediately, I chose to assist him through this rough time. To address his sloppy schoolwork, he was taken off of the basketball and football teams for an indefinite period of time. Both coaches and parents called me during the "rival games" to ask if I would reconsider and allow him to play. Some of the coaches advised me that taking him off of the team for punishment would not be effective. His time on PlayStation and his other fun activities were also removed. To deal with his disrespectful attitude, I took him to the local park (where his friends would gather) and made him pick up the garbage on the playground with a pooper-scooper.

To date, my now fifteen-year-old son is a handsome, respectful, intelligent and athletic young man who is loved by his peers, teachers, and coaches. While he has an occasional relapse and forgets what is expected of him, he understands the concept of consequences. However, as I am typing this manuscript, his eleven-year-old brother is writing in his 150-page spiral notebook "I will do a better job in school."

Discipline is effective when enforced in a consistent manner. It may interfere with family gatherings or other social plans, but it is imperative that parents follow through with the punishment as discussed.

Sexual Activity

Our children have more peer pressure than the generations before them. The progress of technology and the popularity of reality television and music videos create a fantasy world for our children that they are unprepared to handle. Sex is the focus of conversation—from the songs on the radio to the image of celebrities on television engaged in sexual activity that include acts of homosexuality. I have explained to my children that as Muslims, homosexuality is unacceptable and unnatural. I went on to explain that while there is a small percentage of the population whose genetic make-up may cause them to have homosexual or bi-sexual tendencies, the majority of participants are involved because it's "the thing to do." I have explained to my boys that if they are "homosexual" by nature and that is who they are, I will love them unconditionally (I am confident that none of my children are) but compromising their heterosexuality to be accepted by their peers or for any other reason would be selling themselves to the devil.

It's safe to safe that "sex" is the most avoided topic of discussion between parents and their teens. Unfortunately, it is crucial that we provide them with accurate information regarding their sexual development, as doing so may save their lives.

Research shows that teens are experimenting with oral sex at alarming rates. It has been documented that young girls believe that engaging in such activity is safer than having sexual intercourse. We must explain to our children, boys and girls, that this is an act of sex and could result in the spread of sexually transmitted disease. We also want our girls to respect themselves and to understand that their bodies are sacred and should be cherished. This holds true for our boys as well.

Unfortunately, Black boys must be taught the reality of the social system in this country. Unfortunately, they must be taught that there can be damaging consequences for sexual contact with White girls. My son, who started school later than his peers because of his late birthday, will be eighteen-years-old while in his senior year in school. This means that a sexual relationship "gone wrong" could result in false charges against him. While this could be the case with a girl of any race, it is more likely to be taken more seriously if she is White.

Let's review the 2002 case of young Marcus Dixon, an eighteen-year-old high school football player from Rome, Georgia who was charged with aggravated child molestation for having consensual sex with as fifteen-year-old White girl. When she began to fear that her father (a racist) would learn of the relationship, she accused Dixon of rape. She had even confided in a friend her reason for the fabrication and the friend reported this information to authorities. Marcus was a high school senior who boasted a 3.96 GPA and 1200 SAT score. Sadly, he was convicted and sent to prison for several years—resulting in the loss of a college scholarship.

Film maker Keith Beauchamp investigated the suspicious hanging of Raynard Johnson, a high school student from Marion City, Mississippi. Young Mr. Johnson was found in 2000 hanging from a tree by a belt. It was reported that he was dating a White woman who was the relative of a local official. His death was ruled a suicide, and when Mr. Beauchamp requested to review the files from the case, they could not be located.

We would like to believe that cases of lynching are a form of "past day" punishment inflicted upon Black people in our nation's southern states. Beauchamp points out that this is the furthest from the truth. In 2006, sixty-one year old Izelle Parrott was found hanging thirty-five feet in the air from a tree in Glen falls, New York. There were reports that some local whites were upset because Mr. Parrott socialized with several white women from town. Similar to the case of young Raynard Johnson, Mr. Parrott's death was ruled a suicide. Historically speaking, we know that the lynching of Black people was somewhat of a social event for Whites, like a circus or parade. They would gather in large crowds and cheer while Blacks were "strung up and hung until they chocked from lack of oxygen." (Williams, 2003)

While such disturbing and animalistic behavior is not reported as often as it was prior to 1960, it's safe to say such devils still exist and they will continue to protect their White women from Black men "by any means necessary." This topic should be included when discussing "sexual relationships" with Black boys. It could save their lives.

The best age at which to introduce the topic of "sex" should be determined by the parents or guardian. Each child is different and may be prepared for such information at different periods in their lives. However, the introduction of "good and bad touch" should be discussed with children as young as three. In doing so, one could explain the anatomical differences of men and women. This can be done without going into detail.

As we know, once children begin school, they are influenced by others. They begin to learn "slang" for various parts of the body, and this is when parents should intervene. Prior to the onset of puberty, children should be familiar with various aspects of sexual development and sexuality. It is the way we can ensure that they are provided with accurate information. This should include a discussion that focuses on the fact that diseases can be transmitted sexually. We must teach our children that "sex with the wrong person can be fatal." Engaging in such conversation does not encourage premarital sex but it may teach your child to be responsible.

My oldest son and I watched a prime-time special on ABC on teen pregnancy. Our discussion began with a focus on underage sexual activity but turned quickly to a presentation of stereotypes. The story opened with two senior high school students from the northeast. He was Black, she was White. She was a cheerleader he was a popular football player. After months of dating, she became pregnant and he continued with his life as though he had no responsibilities. While she was home, nine months pregnant with the support of her family, he was at the senior prom enjoying the festivities with another girl and did not want to be interviewed. The next story featured a teenage couple from the Midwest, both White, and of course, the young boy was extremely responsible. He worked long hours as a waiter and attended school. Again, her family supported her. The final story focused on a fourteen-year-old Black girl who of course, had no family support as her mother worked long hours and the father of the baby was not a part of her life.

Once again, a discussion on race found its way into our conversation. I had to direct his attention to the fact that as usual, the Black male was placed in the role of the irresponsible teen. The White boy was focused and concerned about the future of his baby and girlfriend. Why couldn't all of the participants in the study be from various racial backgrounds, some victims others not? Also, why did the youngest and most isolated teenager have to be a Black girl?

Preparation for the World

It's imperative that parents understand that children, both boys and girls, need guidance. Recently, I began a series of conversations with my fifteen-year-old who will be old enough to drive next year. I advised him that driving will come with a great deal of responsibilities. Not only will he be expected to be a safe and careful driver, but he will have to be conscious of "driving while Black." He will be profiled racially by both White and Black police officers and a target of "broken" young Black men whose unfortunate set of circumstances may cause them anger and resentment towards another brother who appears to have more. This concern would affect the type of vehicle that he would drive and where he would be permitted to drive it. Certain types and models may be magnets for police. Moreover, one that is too flashy could attract attention from carjackers --- both police and carjackers will shoot to kill.

I went on to inform my son that his choice of friends could cost him a life behind bars. Hill Harper (2006) states that the qualities that you look for in a friend can impact you for a lifetime. The "drop down" of drugs or an illegal weapon on the floor of his car could result in the arrest of the driver and passengers. As I spoke, he looked at me in disbelief and asked, "All of that can happen?" I informed him that it most certainly can happen, as it has happened to many young brothers.

As if the war on drugs is not enough to take our boys out, we also have the World Wide Web as a source of temptation and personal destruction. Often I have advised my children that one stroke of the key can ruin their lives. One does not have to publicize his/her most intimate thoughts or post information that is vulgar and socially unacceptable. Doing so can harm any chances of college scholarships or even career opportunities. For example:

- A Black All-American football player from a Catholic High School in New Jersey was awarded a scholarship to the University of Michigan. He foolishly posted sexual comments on his Twitter page and was expelled from school. As a senior, his opportunities to go to Michigan on a scholarship have been revoked.

- Young girls also must be made aware of the repercussions of such conduct. A nude or semi-nude picture forwarded to a friend can cause major backlash. Parents must be vigilant and discourage children from taking part in cyber behavior that may be damaging to their reputation.

BLACK CHILDREN AND THE SYSTEM OF MIS-EDUCATION

"If a man's not going to treat you right he's not going to
teach you right."
Dr. Jack Felder—Educator

It was 1954 and the ruling of Brown vs. The Board of Education of Topeka Kansas that would alter forever the way in which Black children would be educated in the United States of America. Under the new legislation, Black children had the right and freedom to be integrated into White schools.

While Black parents at the time would believe that sending their children to predominately White schools would provide them with better educational opportunities, we would later learn that this type of education would devastate generations of Black children, particularly boys.

As Black children filtered into the schools normally populated by Whites, it was clear that they were not welcome. The other students, their parents and teachers as well, worked to make the lives of the Black children miserable. The students were viewed as inferior and treated as such by those who were expected to educate them. This inhumane practice would be the foundation of the institution of racism that exists in our schools today. While the laws are less tolerant of overt racism within the schools, Black children are still subjected to discriminatory treatment at the hands of their teachers and those within the educational administration. According to Derrick Bell (1992) it took him awhile to realize that the "integrated schools" were simply comprised of segregated educational programs—one for White children the other for Blacks. The Black students did not have Black teachers or administrators and were disciplined for any behavior believed to be threatening to White students.

By the 1980's President Ronald Reagan worked diligently to undo any progress that benefited Black students prior to his term in office. This included the appointment of racist Bill Bennett as Secretary of Education. In 2005 Mr. Bennett proposed that "all Black children be aborted in order to reduce crime." What effect did his belief about Black children have on his decision-making ability concerning their education?

Several years ago, I interviewed a seventy-five year old woman, Ms. Judy, about her experiences going to grade school in Freehold, New Jersey, one of the last school districts to integrate voluntarily. She described her time at the one room school house as "something to remember." She explained that the local elementary school across the street from her home was for White children only and that she had to walk over three miles each day to and from the segregated one room schoolhouse.

Ms. Judy describes her teacher as a woman who cared about the students. The teacher was responsible for educating children of different ages. This was second nature. She was committed to improving the lives of the children during a time when the White establishment didn't feel as though they were worthy of quality education. She talked about the old tattered and outdated books that she and her peers were expected to use. She recalled nights when the weather was so poor that the teacher would spend the night in the school building because she feared that it would be difficult for her to get to the school the next day. Ms. Judy recalled feeling a sense of commitment and concern from her teacher.

One could only imagine the outcome of many generations of Black students if the segregated one-room school house had never been dismantled. We would have more leverage as citizens in the United States, as our value system and sense of pride and cohesiveness would be more prominent as we would fight to maintain our legacy. Many of the little Black boys who performed so poorly in public schools throughout the nation over the last sixty years would have been saved. They would have had teachers who cared about them and expected only the best performance. Such influential schools would have resulted in powerful neighborhoods, thus altering our position within the social fabric of the country.

Fifty-five years after Brown vs. the Board of Education, Black students have not been accepted into the White system of education. Public schools throughout the country are as segregated as they were prior to the court ruling. White families are enrolling their children in private schools, forming charter schools, or even moving out of more diverse school districts so that their children can attend schools populated by White students. To date, many activists understand that rather than fighting for integration, Blacks should have fought for "separate but equal" educational opportunities.

This dilemma with Black students within the school system involves children from all socioeconomic backgrounds. Many White teachers have stereotypical views of their Black students, regardless of the economic background of their parents. Unfortunately, those children who are from socially deprived households with no parents to speak on their behalf are more likely to become victimized.

Secretary of Education, Arne Duncan, commented on the rebirth of the New Orleans's school district by stating "Hurricane Katrina was the best thing that happened for the students of New Orleans." He went on to explain that because of "Katrina" an inadequate and non-functioning school district was reorganized and the children could now receive an education comparable to that found in other parts of the country. Why do Black children have to experience such tragedy in order to receive the same educational services as their White counterparts? Is there any concern about the psychological wellbeing of these children after they survived the vicious flood? Or after many of them witnessed their parents or loved ones brutalized at the hands of the police during the aftermath of Katrina? Would Mr. Duncan have the same philosophical belief if the youngest victims of "the flood" were blond-haired and blue-eyed?

The key to a successful system of education is to have a concern for the population being educated. We know that the lives of Black children are not valued in our country, but the amount of federal money provided based on their attendance in school is. School administrators understand that they can provide substandard education and receive the same funding as do other districts. Teachers in New York City can obtain a license to teach without studying Black history. How can a teacher teach "history" without understanding the historical events surrounding the arrival of Black people in the United States?

In 1992 researcher Jonathan Kozol documented his findings as a teacher in a district in Boston populated by Black children. He reported that Black children were at the forefront of mistreatment while in school. He described the classrooms as over-crowded and reported that the teachers attacked the self-esteem of students through the use of racist books and educational tools as well as imposing violent and inappropriate methods of discipline. Kozol went on to report that Black students were viewed as "stupid" and were less likely to succeed than their White counterparts. As he began to prove his colleagues wrong in their approach to the education of Black children, he was fired.

Such emotional and intellectual abuse was not limited to the school district of Boston, but was rather commonplace in both the inner-city and the suburbs. Freiere (1998) reminds us that children are aware of the injustices of which they are faced in school and sometimes respond by ending their schooling. We know that the typical drop-out is one who is struggling in class and feeling a sense of helplessness.

> "In reality, we do not have children who drop out of school for no reason at all, as if they just decided not to stay. What we do have are conditions in schools that either prevent them from coming to school or prevent them from staying in school." (Freire, p. 6)

Preschool

We often think that educational tracking begins at the formal stages of schooling. This is not the case, as Black children (particularly boys) are often placed on the "poor behavior track" prior to entering kindergarten.

Since 1991, I have had hundreds of Black boys enroll in my preschool program after having been terminated from various predominately White establishments. Some parents were convinced that their sons were behaviorally problematic and in need of medicinal assistance in order to control behavior that the teachers described as out of control, while others believed that the behavior that their children exhibited was over scrutinized by teachers as conduct similar by White boys went unnoticed. In most of the cases the teachers had diagnosed these boys with Attention Deficit Disorder with Hyperactivity and recommended that they seek psychological services.

In 2001, I requested that fifteen of the families complete a questionnaire that focused on the type of program that the child attended previously. All of the fifteen schools were operated by a White female director and only two of the schools had even one Black teacher. Four of the schools were populated by a small percentage of Black children while the other eleven included five or fewer Black children.

It seemed that the common factor throughout the fifteen schools was their lack of sensitivity towards their Black male students. The fact that teachers were permitted to evaluate the psychological and educational status of a child is of great concern. The only professional qualified to produce a psychological or intellectual evaluation is a licensed psychologist or psychiatrist. The fact that ninety-eight percent of the boys enrolled into my program continued for two years trouble-free and move successfully through their formal schooling led me to believe that the current environment was the cause of the misbehavior, if in fact any misbehavior had really occurred at all.

Early childhood is the period when children are most impressionable. They become what we believe them to be. These boys could have been scarred for life had they continued their schooling in an environment that was not only insensitive to their needs but racist.

To date, many of our two and three-year-old boys are viewed as behaviorally challenged and intellectually inferior by many day care providers and specialists. I have experienced such mistreatment from the White teachers working within my program. I noticed that their lack of sensitivity towards our children interferes with how they treat them. For instance, I watched as three four-year-old Black girls volunteered to help a White teacher place the mats on the floor for nap time. As their little arms carried three bags each filled with blankets and pillows, the teacher ordered them to take the bags in the other room. As they brushed passed the teacher, she informed one of the girls that the bags that she was carrying hit her on the leg. Immediately, I advised the teacher that as the adult, she was to praise the girls for volunteering to help. I also stated that a "thank you" was also in order. I explained that this is how children develop a sense of pride and self-esteem. This experience was symbolic of the treatment that is imposed upon our children in predominately White schools.

As Black parents, we continue to try to assimilate into White culture as we choose to enroll our children in preschool programs that provide all of the "things" that we believe make for a healthy environment such as: a state of the art computer lab and gym room. One must remember that young children require the basics in order to flourish—a clean, safe, healthy environment rooted in structure, discipline and love. Those young children who have the opportunity to experience such a program will be prepared to master their formal schooling.

Pre-kindergarten

Pre-kindergarten is the stage just before kindergarten. It is the period in education that prepares children for their formal schooling. The most common complaint that I hear from parents as relevant to their pre-kindergartner's education is the "cut-off" date for entering kindergarten as set by each school district at the local level. This policy is usually aggravating for many parents, particularly if their child's birthday is several days shy of the specific date. Some parents however, are thankful for the extra time their children will have to prepare for school. These are often White parents who understand the advantage of allowing their children to repeat pre-kindergarten. It is we, the Black parents, who once again are three paces behind.

Many do not realize the impact that one month has on the cognitive development of a four—year—old. One may believe that a four-year-old child whose birthday is October 1st should be permitted to attend school even if the child should have been five by September 1st. Premature enrollment can impede a child's ability to learn. Young children are maturing each day. While a few weeks may not be significant developmentally to an older child, it is to a child who is younger.

The advantage of delayed kindergarten entry enables the child to mature socially and obtain the tools necessary to progress from one stage of development to the next. This includes the ability to perform strongly on standardized tests. While White parents have been cognizant of this practice, we Black parents are more concerned with how their children are viewed by others if they start kindergarten late, rather than what's most beneficial. A five-year-old will harbor no hard feelings or be affected by repeating pre-kindergarten. They don't recognize "kindergarten" as the start of formal schooling. It's when the child is retained once he or she has started school that damage may be done to self-confidence, as the young child watches friends move to the next grade.

Kindergarten

Once our children begin kindergarten, the formal practice of labeling and tracking begins, particularly for our Black boys. Their file becomes the vehicle for their educational collapse.

In 2007, Black Women Against Racism (BWARE) publicized a conspiracy by a White female principal of a kindergarten program in a suburban community outside of New York City, who attempted to keep seventy-five kindergarten children (mostly Black) from moving to the first grade. Her excuse was that they were not able to read, even though research has proven that while there are some children who do learn before age six, reading readiness begins in kindergarten and fluent reading is accomplished at the end of grade one. Her scheme was to restructure the program through the use of "inclusion" which would incorporate those children with special needs into the typical classroom. The general education teacher would then be expected to adapt to a classroom dynamic that would include children that he or she has not been trained to teach. Even though an assistant would be added, this would indeed increase the classroom size and the student-teacher ratio.

This proposal was so bizarre that we spent several months investigating the facts. We could not rationalize the choice to revamp an entire program that would involve retaining older students and blending those with special needs into the classroom setting. This woman was able to modify an entire school without the approval of the local Board of Education or Superintendent of Schools. None of the administrators were concerned with her conduct since this was a district populated by Black and Brown children.

We would later learn that the principal's choice to modify the curriculum was supported for two reasons. The population in this specific kindergarten program had been on the decline, as many of the families in the district had chosen religious schools or the charter program which would explain the high rate of retention among those who remained in the system. We also discovered that the principal, a Doctoral candidate was working on her dissertation, which focused on teaching techniques similar to her plans for the program. We did report our findings to both the state and federal Board of Education. While most of the children moved forward to first grade, there was no further investigation by the board into whether this principal had violated any code of ethics. She was eventually transferred, and her program dismantled.

Black children continue to be "at risk" while enrolled in their school settings. It is imperative that parents and community activists maintain a presence so that school administrators and local officials are aware that they are under the microscope at all times. But while we monitor members of the White establishment, we must remember that there are Black teachers who have no loyalty to the Black student and considers him a failure. This sense of self-hatred contributes to the conspiracy to destroy our children.

When my five-year-old son began kindergarten, I was permitted to select a teacher since I was paying for him to attend a school outside of our district. After several telephone calls to educators with whom I was friendly, I was encouraged to select an older African-American woman who had worked in the district for many years. Of course this was exciting for me, as I believe in the approach of teaching and discipline as implemented by our elders.

Several days before school we were to take our children to the classroom to meet the teacher. When the teacher realized that we were the family from Paterson, New Jersey, she immediately informed me that she provides remedial classes for those children who are somewhat delayed. I went on to inform her that my son had been enrolled in my program since he was an infant and that he was well prepared for kindergarten.

Each day, I would wait with my son in the hallway until the teacher arrived. I was not comfortable with the fact that twenty, five-year-old children were left unattended in the hallway. I would usually attempt to organize the group as some of the boys played roughly. Once the teacher arrived, I noticed that she would always discipline the little Black boys who were running around, never addressing their White counterparts who behaved in the same manner. I would inform her that *all* of the boys were misbehaving, probably because they were unsupervised.

Several weeks later, my son came home and said "I can't do anything right. The teacher put me in the slow reading group. Dan (a little White boy) is in the fast group because she tells him that he's the best reader. She has him read for the class every day." My heart dropped to my feet. I had spent five years ensuring that my child's self-confidence and self-esteem were developed, and this woman destroyed it in a matter of weeks. I was concerned that a five-year-old was aware that he was in a slower-tracked group. A caring teacher would never categorize children in such a way that they could determine in which level he had been placed.

After two weeks of continued problems that appeared to be racially motivated in the favor of the two White boys in the class, my husband and I contacted the principal and requested to have our child removed from this teacher's class. Several days later, four of the other Black boys were too removed. I realized that my son, one of five fair-skinned Black boys, seemed to be the target of this teacher's wrath. She, a dark skinned woman in her early sixties, clearly had issues regarding skin color among little Black boys. She allowed her past to interfere with her ability to teach.

This is a sad case of reality. We must be suspicious not only of the White teachers but also of the Black educators, as well. We as parents must advocate for our children without feeling a sense of intimidation.

Primary School

Prior to my own children beginning school, several friends warned me to be prepared to deal with the institution of racism within the school system. I did not understand fully their advice until my two boys started school. What a nightmare it has been. Most of teachers in the classroom with our children are young White women who most likely have never interacted with Black people and have no knowledge of our history. How can they teach effectively a group of whom they know nothing about?

One damp rainy Monday, I left work to attend an awards assembly in which my eight-year-old would participate. When I arrived, my son was walking back to his seat after receiving an award for "best sportsmanship." The teacher then went on to announce that she would now present her own personal token to the students according to their performance during the year. I watched as each child was given an award for an achievement that related to his or her academic accomplishments. I assumed that since my child was a straight "A" student who continually received praise from the teacher for his wonderful demeanor and compliant behavior, that he would be considered for something "meaningful." Of course I would be wrong as my child, the only Black boy in the classroom, would receive an award for "most athletic."

Listening in disbelief, I sat as still as a board, attempting to process this act that I found to be insulting, insensitive, and even racist. On what basis was he given this award? He did not participate in any team sports in school and there is no playground where he could have exhibited his athletic abilities. Frustrated and angry, I contacted the principal and informed her of my concern. I went on to revisit my request from the previous year that the teachers be required to complete a diversity training course. The principal was perplexed by my concerns and did not feel that the teacher's decision was inappropriate.

After this futile discussion, the teacher contacted me in an attempt to state her case. She explained how she spent the entire evening before reviewing each child's performance so that she could best select the proper award. I asked her how she determined that my son was so athletic when their playground consisted of "a parking lot." She informed me that she saw him run and participate in a number of activities during field day and she was so impressed with his coordination and ability to run and jump. I replied, "So my child's one day of athletic performance was more impressive to you than his entire year as a straight A student?" The teacher continued that she did not believe her choice to be as serious as I had claimed and that she thought my son was excited to receive such acknowledgement. I had to decipher for her the stereotypical beliefs related to Black boys, highlighting the belief that Black boys can only excel in sports. She said that she viewed all of children as "the same." I told her that she was doing them a disservice because they were not the same.

At the end of the conversation she asked, "What is it that you would like me to do?" I told her that I wanted her to give him an award that recognized his "well-roundedness." She accepted my request. The next day when I arrived to get my son from school, he announced, "Guess what, Mommy?! I got another award today. It was for being the most well-rounded." He was so excited. I went on to remind him of how proud I was of all of his accomplishments.

Middle School

By grade five or so, our beautiful Black boys begin to look like young men. They no longer bear the baby face that reminds us of young childhood but rather the "face of danger" as viewed by members of the White establishment, particularly White females who teach in many of our classrooms.

According to Jawanza Kunjufu (1983) Black boys begin to dislike school by grade four. Kunjufu continues to discuss how their appearances affect the way that they are viewed by their teachers. Children are intuitive and can sense when they are disliked. Such a barrier between teacher and student results in the breakdown of learning.

In September 2007, a school in New Jersey was featured on the news when a White teacher assigned her sixth grade class to assume the role as "plantation owner" and organize an argument as to why their plantation was the most effective and how their slaves would be more effective. As usual, the NAACP requested an apology rather than demanding the termination of the teacher and requiring sensitivity training for those remaining. Members and supporters of BWARE demanded the latter. There was a letter writing campaign put into place, as well as a telephone call placed to the office of the superintendent who seemed to be concerned and apologetic but did not agree that the teacher should be fired.

Over the last several years, I have worked with several middle-school boys in one suburban neighborhood who were considering home-schooling as opposed to attending public school. In one such case, the parents of a fourteen-year-old boy contacted me because he no longer wanted to go to school. A well-liked boy with many friends was not comfortable in class. On our first meeting, I was greeted by a tall, handsome boy who appeared somewhat shy. Thirty minutes into the conversation he informed me that he had always maintained good grades but those grades declined once he entered grade eight. One of his teachers did not view him as worthwhile. She, an older White woman would not even say good morning when he spoke. He went on to say that she only acknowledged him when he provided a wrong answer or didn't do well on a test. The most heart-wrenching moment was when this six foot something boy broke down in tears and stated, "They never even say have a good day at the end of class." Here was a boy from an upper-middle class family who had the luxury of traveling and living in the grand suburbs of New York but was so unhappy with his educational experience that he did not want to return to school—simply because he was not made to feel important or worthwhile by his White female teachers.

It is for this reason that we have to consider carefully the educational path our children will travel. When selecting an area to live and raise our children, it is imperative that we consider the community's school system. As Black people have become more educated and have experienced financial success we are anxious to live among the affluent, usually White communities without considering the schools that our children will attend.

At one point, all three of my children were enrolled in a Catholic school. As a Muslim, a Catholic school was my last resort. While my oldest was enrolled for several years in public school, I felt that he needed an environment that was smaller, more structured, and rooted in discipline. Nevertheless, we always face a dilemma, that of racism, when dealing with our Black children in school.

This particular school was populated by a large Hispanic and Black community. The principal was White, as were all of the teachers except one. While the tone of the school mimicked a "close knit family," it was clear that *the family* was White. On several occasions I had to remind the principal and several of the teachers that the school was comprised of children of color—not reflected in the population of teachers in the school. In addition, the teachers were not well versed in American history, as they continued to provide misinformation concerning the history of African-Americans in the United States or ignore their contributions completely.

After the election of Barack Obama, in 2008, I suggested to the principal and several of the teachers that I thought it was important that the students understand the importance of the election from a historical point of view. I felt that they should know the history of Black people and their struggle to gain the right to vote in this country. One of the teachers informed me that she had explained to her class that "Black people couldn't vote because they couldn't read or write." Imagine the pain that traveled down my neck and back when hearing this? Politely, but in a firm voice, I expressed my concern that she was providing false information to the students. I went on to explain to her that there were many Black intellectuals who could read and write but who had been murdered, raped and hanged for expressing their right to vote.

While this particular Catholic school focused on discipline but not history as relevant to Black people, another institution where my oldest son had also been enrolled was a charter school ten miles away and was the opposite. The school, small in size, was located in a New York City suburban community and populated by Black boys. It was operated by a Black doctoral-level female and directed by her superior, a White male. The school curriculum was rich in culture as it focused on the contributions of Black people to the history of the United State. Such an approach to learning is critical for self-esteem and development. However, the one component missing from this program was the implementation of effective disciplinary practices.

During one particular school year, there were several complaints that a group of boys were continually sent to the principal's office for rough behavior during free play. Parents confessed that they sat in their cars during lunch to witness sixty boys or so fighting over one ball, while the four teachers who were supposed to supervise the activities were yards away from where the boys played.

When this concern was brought to the attention of the principal and the director, the director commented, "Well, boys will be boys, and it's normal for them to visit the principal." While "boys will be boys," it is not acceptable for them to be sent to the office each day. Black boys must be prepared for the world. They should not be permitted to behave in a manner that is socially unacceptable while in school or elsewhere for that matter.

Middle school is an important phase of education for children. The work becomes more challenging and there is an increase in the number of standardized tests that are administered throughout their schooling. Through experience with my own children, I have learned that we Black parents have to subsidize the learning that our children receive. If they are not receiving something at school, we must provide it at home.

As a single mother, I make *every* experience a tool for teaching my children. One afternoon, as my ten-year-old son and his classmates participated in a basketball game against a predominately White school from Elmwood Park, New Jersey, I had to sit and watch the referees (two older White men) make favorable calls for the White boys so that our children of color had no chance of winning. Whenever our team began to win, the cheating began. Once they began to lose dramatically, the referees began to make legitimate calls. This act of racism was so obvious that my son and his teammates began to feel defeated. Some wept and lost their sense of confidence as they played, while others became filled with anger. I yelled to my son, "Keep going . . . their plan is to break your spirit . . . this is what they do in real life!"

After the game, I explained to my boys that they had experienced the institutional racism about which I constantly spoke. I went on to say that the game was symbolic of what they will experience as Black boys and men for the rest of their lives. The White boys (who were no better than our boys) were full of confidence as they played because they knew that they had a support system in the referees and coaches. They begin with an advantage. This is exactly what happens in real life. White children (no better than others) have the confidence and self-esteem needed to develop fully. Since life will not be fair to my Black boys, they have to be better and work harder because as they move forward, there will be someone to discriminate against them because of the color of their skin. It's those who are unprepared who are defeated in the end.

High School

High school is the last phase of formal mis-education to which our children will be exposed. Those who complete successfully the last three or four years of public school will have demonstrated great endurance. Many fail to realize that the high school level is more difficult and may present deeper issues of racism and disregard for the Black student. Black boys now look like Black men—most feared by their young White female teachers who have absolutely nothing in common with them. If they were lucky to have a teacher who was nurturing and caring in their younger grades, chances are they no longer have such guidance. This neglect is not limited to boys. Black girls are also affected while they are experiencing their own struggles. They compete with their White female counterparts who have assumed their role in the classroom as "most valuable." White female teachers can relate to them as they remind them of themselves or their daughters. White men worship them as one day they will develop into White women—the most treasured possession of them all.

The most disturbing example of neglect and disregard for life within any school system of which I am familiar, occurred in April 2007 at Teaneck High School, when a group of students were taken on a trip to Africa by several teachers. Several days into the trip, a sixteen-year-old student named Phylicia Moore was found dead floating in the hotel pool. Once reported to the school district, the superintendent (White male), called the girl's father at work and reported this devastating news. The superintendent, the mayor (Jewish male) and the school principal (Black female) found it acceptable for the trip to continue. I am 99.9% sure that if this were a White girl from the community who was on an international trip with her school, the trip would have been discontinued and everyone would have been ordered to return to the States. Oddly, many of the Black residents from Teaneck were disturbed by Mr. and Mrs. Moore's decision to continue the investigation into their daughter's murder. Members of Black Women Against Racism were met with resistance during the twenty days that they protested in front of city hall.

The body of young Phylicia was sent back to the states and the students and their chaperones continued their trip as though the student were a piece of luggage. Once again, would this have been the response if Phylicia were a White student? In fact, we have the example of Natalee Hollaway, who disappeared while on a school trip to Aruba. Authorities discovered that Ms. Holloway had been drinking and had left her classmates to go with two male strangers whom she met at the bar. Ms. Hollaway's classmates did not discover that she was missing until they arrived at the airport. Ms. Moore was known as a quiet student who would not have jeopardized her safety as did Ms. Holloway—but still, Ms. Holloway's life was viewed as more valuable.

While this is an extreme case of educational disservice towards Black teenage students by the White system of education, it does demonstrate the depth of complete disregard for the overall well being of our children.

Since high school is the last phase of formal schooling required by the United States Department of Education, Black parents must continue their involvement in their child's schooling. The performance of the high school student will determine his or her success as a young adult. If our students are not provided the appropriate guidance by their teachers and counselors, we need to intervene. In many cases, Black parents are not involved and oftentimes too intimidated to question educators.

We are usually accepting of educational reports that feature specific schools that have been given the "blue ribbon award for performance" or have been documented as higher scoring on standardized tests than other schools. We are so eager to enroll our children in such institutions that we do so without considering the many other factors. In some cases, a good school that may not appear to be high performing may have a large number of non-English speaking students affecting test scores. Moreover, schools may misreport their scores to attain a high ranking. Several years ago it was reported that Fort Lee High School in Fort Lee, New Jersey, listed as one of the top high schools in the nation, had received this honor based on falsified test scores and grades. It is safe to say that this unethical and illegal practice is commonplace within the schools of our country. Cheating and lying is as American as apple pie, and we must understand that the White media emphasizes the problems within the inner-city schools and downplays the corruption within those schools populated by White students. The lesson is simple --- "don't believe every report written about us or them."

Cultural School

Those from other groups have migrated to the United States and formed their own enclaves throughout the country. Their focus seems to concentrate on how best to benefit from the educational opportunities offered while maintaining their cultural values and traditions. This is most noticeable amongst the Japanese who operate "Japanese class" for their children as young as three-years-old. These programs operate all-year-around and are usually held on Saturdays.

Such cultural exposure is essential to the development of self-esteem and pride. Children should know from where they come and the importance of embracing traditional practices as done so by ancestors. Cultural schooling for African-American children would allow them the opportunity to learn about their heritage while in the company of those like them—creating a sense of belonging.

Mentors

It's horrifying to hear an unconscious educated brother attempt to "school" young Black boys. During my discussion with members of the football team in Paterson, New Jersey, several educators, were invited to speak to a group of 12, 13, and 14 year-old boys. The tone of the lecture from several of the speakers was "You get straight A's and you can get into any Ivy League school of your choice."

It was disturbing to listen to *my successful brothers* advise these boys that their success or failure depended on whether or not they were accepted into an Ivy League University. The message was "pull yourselves up by your bootstraps and you'll be fine." One speaker grew up in the ghetto but completed three degrees at Harvard. He went on to ask the boys which ones had earned straight A's. When many of the boys admitted that they had not received A's, he went on to say that "as you get older your grades go down because you are more focused on other things." He failed to acknowledge the fact that studies show that by grade four, the academic performance of Black boys tends to decrease because they begin to resemble Black men, a group most feared by White women. He failed to explain how it was important to "do your best" and get into college, whether it be to an Ivy League institution, historically Black college, or a community college.

While an Ivy League education would be beneficial to the careers of some Black children, it is not a realistic goal. Every child will not be an "A" student. Students should be encouraged to strive for excellence and should understand that being average does not indicate failure.

My experience as an activist and an early educational psychologist has provided me with important insight into the belief system of the Black parent as relevant to the child's education. We often associate success with predominately White institutions. I continually advise parents to enroll their children in educational institutions where they can thrive and not feel as though they don't belong.

Educational Field Trips

As a child of the 1980's, I remember clearly the field trips taken to the landmarks in New York City that I found to be most boring. These excursions had no relevance to my life as a Black child. There was no discussion of the contributions from my people, those who could have been my great-great grandfather or great-great grandmother. That type of exposure would have allowed me a sense of pride as a young Black girl.

Dr. Joy DeGruy brings to light this deception as woven into the fabric of this country, as she lectured on the history of the Statue of

Liberty. She explains that the statue originally held chains in her left hand to represent the end of slavery. Members of the establishment in the U.S. did not want the chains included, so they requested that they be removed. The French artist agreed to replace the chains with tablets but refused to shed the chains as they represented "freedom" in a land of the free. The chains were then moved to the bottom of statue's feet and can only be seen if one is flying above in a plane or helicopter.

During a visit to the statue, Dr. DeGruy listened and observed as the tour guide gave a detailed account of the history of the statue to groups of school children. After his discussion, she quietly asked the guide to explain the significance of the chains. According to Dr. DeGruy, he appeared to be shocked that she made reference to the symbol and then went on to discuss the significance. Why was that not included as information necessary to present an accurate account of the statue's history?

Dr. DeGruy had a similar experience when visiting Ellis Island. She described how she walked through a room called the "peopling room." This room featured a chart of all the immigrants that migrated through. Included was an area entitled "legend" that included "non-voluntary immigrants," which included Africans. There was no discussion about the impact and process of slavery. There was no discussion about genocide or the Atlantic slave trade. There were pictures of the sleeping quarters of immigrants that showed hammocks and sinks. Where was the picture of the slave ship that transported thousands of Africans during one trip chained next to one another in fecal waste and bodily fluids? Dr. DeGruy goes on to ask why are we expected to feel the pain of Europeans, but White descendants of these Europeans are not expected to feel the pain of slaves? Even though Ellis Island chronicles only those who entered the country there, some form of documentation should have described the tragedy of slavery.

As we remembered those who lost their lives on September 11, 2001, I can't help to notice that there is no discussion of the three Black students from Washington DC who won a contest to participate in a science fair sponsored by National Geographic, when their plane (flight 77) crashed into The Pentagon. I can't help to think that if these students were White, their story would have been told on a national level.

When I contacted the three schools from where the students had come, I informed the administrators that I was a researcher and I was attempting to gather information regarding the students. I went on to say that I was concerned that the stories of these children had not been told. The administrators from each school were pleased with the coverage and informed me that this information was televised on all of the local channels and printed in the local newspapers. Was that enough? Why wasn't this worthy of national news? We know the answer—the students were Black.

THE DILEMMA
OF THE BLACK MALE

"People judge me according to their circumstances
instead of judging me according to my own."
T.I.—Lyricist, Rapper

On September 12, 2011 while driving with two of my children, I was stopped behind a public transportation bus at a traffic light. I was forced to read an enormous billboard posted on the back of the bus that boasted of the "excellence" within the Bergen County school system. The placard featured five children—four Whites (boys and girls) and one Black girl. My eleven-year-old son said, "Look mommy, there are no Black boys in that picture." It saddened me that my son realized that he wasn't included in the presentation of high quality education. I explained to him that this was an example of how White society works diligently to exclude Black boys and men from anything meaningful. I went on to remind him that Black people can be part of the conspiracy as the county superintendent is a Black man.

The Black male is the cornerstone of the Black community. His role as husband, father, son and mentor sets the tone for the progression and development of self-determination that is critical to the productive growth of any group of people. While there are those brothers who understand their responsibilities and take seriously their role as head of household and leader within the community, there are those who do not. Their lack of concern and responsibility continues to devastate the Black family unit. Today's Black boy must be prepared to function as a husband/partner and father within a White racist society.

Historically, the plan was to make Black men feel worthless and inferior through the use of physical and psychological torture. Their captors would work vigorously to damage their dignity and shatter their souls. Fortunately, many Black men were able to overcome this conspiracy, as they would go on as free men on a mission to provide for their families. But those in power would once again challenge their manhood.

While slavery ended officially in 1865, economic slavery began through sharecropping. Blacks rented land, bought food on credit, and borrowed equipment and paid inflated prices for necessities. Illiterate men signed unfair contracts, and they would fall into debt and then be imprisoned. White men had the option to pay the slaves' debt in full in exchange for labor that would continue until the loan was repaid. It's not surprising that at harvest time, there would be an increase in the number of Black men arrested and jailed for loitering and drunkenness simply so that White folks had their choice of men to work for them privately.

Caught in a system of violence and corruption, an overwhelmingly number of Black men have fallen prey to drugs in the USA—heroin, marijuana, cocaine and crack. Either they are addicts or have become pimps for White men who are at the helm of this network. If these brothers were familiar with their history, they would understand that they have been the target of the establishment for over four hundred years.

I began advocating for Black boys in 1991 when I realized that the "conspiracy to destroy Black boys," as theorized by Jawanza Kunjufu, was accurate—the number of Black boys in special education classes increased as well as did the number of those who were incarcerated. I began to believe that the plan was institutionalized.

Speaking from a historical context once again, there are a number of reasons that Black men would leave their homes. Many Black folks were poor and received financial assistance. The law required that the head of household not be present in order for the woman to be eligible. The women were forced to raise their Black boys without the support of the father. Some were successful in doing so, while others were not.

For decades, we accepted the theory advanced by scholars, Black and White, that the absence of the Black father in the home has resulted in generations of Black boys who would not obtain the tools necessary to adjust to the responsibilities of manhood. The approach to parenting as implemented by the mother (whether the father was present or not) was not considered. As a mother of two Black sons and a daughter, my interest in the mother-son relationship is not an attempt to diminish the significance of the role of the Black father, but rather to focus on the role of the mother and provide suggestions on how she can better prepare her son. The Black boy will one day become a Black man, eventually (in most cases) becoming a husband and father and continuing the cycle to which he has been exposed. If his childhood experience was productive, then he will employ a similar approach in his relationships. If it was not, it will be difficult for him to form healthy relationships.

Relationship with Dad

All of America is aware that the Black father is absent from the household in large numbers. It's a topic of discussion on which every media outlet has focused its attention. There are very few studies that highlight the effective Black fathers who take the role as head of household seriously, which is why the intention is not to focus on stereotypes but rather to discuss those approaches that may enhance the relationship between father and son.

There is no relationship more critical to the productive growth of the Black boy than his connection to his father. Black boys need to feel a sense of security and to have someone to emulate. Feelings of rejection by one's father may result in behaviors which are self-destructive and/ or antisocial, thus interfering with the Black boy's progression into manhood.

A meaningful father-son relationship requires Dad to develop a foundation with his boy from birth and continue to be involved during childhood, not only during athletic activities but as the boy progresses through his education and his social life. Doing so will create a special bond like no other, enabling Dad to understand his son as he grows. While most men (regardless of race) usually are more interested in their boys' athletic abilities, Black folks can't do as do others. Since our families are at risk, as a preemptive approach, Black fathers have to opt for alternative approaches of parenting.

Black boys are in dire need of guidance and modeling from their fathers or male role models. Their needs are different from those of their female counterparts. Black boys must be groomed to become men and must be prepared to one day provide for a wife and children. It is the Black father who has the tools (hopefully) to help the boy(s) at this point. It is *he* whom the Black boy will respect and trust for advice.

Men who are either detached from their boys or choose to be uninvolved are contributing to a generation of young Black men who exhibit a sense of low self-esteem and self-worth. These young men go on to become mates and fathers of their own boys—and the cycle continues.

The Bond with Mom

The bond between mother and son is also important. She is the first caregiver, teacher, and woman in his life. He is the innocent brown boy who will one day belong to the most feared group of people in the world.

A young woman who had just given birth to her first baby, a boy, asked me who was easier to raise, my daughter or my sons. When I answered my daughter, she was shocked. She informed me that all of her friends believed their sons to be easier than their daughters. I responded, "That's the problem. Black women believe that raising sons is less complicated than raising girls because we are not doing our job with our boys." Anyone who says that raising a Black boy is easy, is not preparing the Black boy to be a Black man. While most of my friends were eager to give birth to boys, I cried when learning the gender of my first two children (both boys) because I understood this reality and the challenges they would face.

case one

A male friend was raised as though he were a privileged White boy. While he was raised comfortably, he is not White. His mother, a domineering Black woman who seemed to identify with working class White people, believed this affiliation placed her in a category superior to that of her Black counterparts, no matter the social class. His father, a pleasant man, allowed his wife to run the household as he served as an onlooker. The style of parenting as implemented by his wife was based on the White child psychologist from the 1960's, Dr. Spock. The focus for her little Black boy was his mother's concern for how things appeared to others rather than instilling a sense of self-esteem or self-respect in her son.

While his father was present in his life, his mother was in charge. He was taught that his good looks would open doors without any effort from him. His mother believed that his athletic ability would be the key to his success. Unfortunately, my friend would never attain the tools that he needed to develop into a man. He has struggled through life unable to take full control of his own household because he was simply not prepared to do so.

case two

While an overbearing mother can stifle her son's ability to develop into a productive man, the neglectful mother can interfere with her son's ability to experience meaningful relationships with others.

An older male relative's dysfunctional relationship with the Black women in his life can be traced back to the hurtful relationship with his mother.

The middle child of three boys, my relative was sent down south to live with his grandmother at a very young age as his mother could not care for all three boys. She, an attractive woman, was a woman of leisure and needed time to socialize. Eventually, she shipped her eldest son to her mother allowing the youngest boy to remain with her.

During manhood, my relative relocated north where he began a family of his own. His mother would soon move several blocks from him. As she aged, he became her sole provider as the other siblings lived at a distance. She, a strong-willed and controlling woman, would speak to her son as though he were a child. He was so intimidated that he would never challenge her but rather fill up with resentment towards her until the day that she died.

To date, my relative has estranged relationships with most of the Black women in his life.

case three

The problem is not always the absent Black father, as many scholars have led us to believe, but rather the mother who chooses to worship her son rather than to raise him. This choice creates a "man child," who does not have the tools to make the transition into manhood.

Through informal discussions with married and divorced women, I have learned that many have implemented a form of mothering with their spouses rather than a partnership in which the man provides for her and assumes the role of protector. In most of these cases, the husband was raised in a household with a mother who worshipped him as though he were God himself. This twisted relationship usually begins in early childhood—so deeply rooted that it interfered with the maturation process for the "Black prince." Once in his own household, he has proven to be incompetent and unable to act as head of household, relying on his wife for strength and everything else.

All but one of the women with whom I spoke felt as though their husbands were weak and did not represent what they believed to be a strong Black man. While three had good relationships with their mothers-in-law, all believed that their mate's mother contributed to her son's inability to be an effective provider.

After School Programs

Black children in our inner-cities and Black communities have suffered most from the lack of resources utilized to fund after school programs. Such programs afford children a safe place to do homework, socialize, and partake in extracurricular activities while under adult supervision. Typically, school districts populated by children of color don't have such access due to budget cuts and/or the misappropriation of funds. However, when there is such a program, it rarely receives media coverage.

The Teaneck Terpsichoreans is a modern dance club founded by Cheryl Miller-Porter in 1971. Mrs. Porter, a graduate of Hampton University began the dance group as "The Teaneck Modern Dance Club." The students both male and female are trained by professional dancers and choreographers in technical and creative dance. The dancers are required to maintain an average grade point in order to participate. An annual performance is held in February during Black history month. The dancers also travel down south to perform at high schools and Historical Black Colleges and Universities.

Over the next forty years, the troupe would graduate thousands of young dancers. Some would go on to become professional dancers or studio owners while others continued on in other professions. The standard under which the members would behave was paramount. We were expected to behave as respectable young men and women while in school or out in the community.

In February 2011 I had the honor of performing in the 40 year reunion show with dozens of my old classmates. As I watched the high school performers from backstage, I was moved to see star football and basketball players participate in this joyous occasion as male dancers. These young talented Black boys were not afraid to exhibit their emotional side as they moved together to spiritual tunes that brought the audience to tears. These boys could be "hanging out" after school, but the dance company afforded the opportunity to be productive instead.

MISSING WOMAN—BLACK

"I am preoccupied with the spiritual survival, the survival
whole of my people. But beyond that, I am committed to
exploring the oppressions, the loyalties, and the triumph
of Black women . . . for me, Black women are the most
fascinating creatures in the world."
Alice Walker—Author

Ironically, while typing this chapter, I could hear the morning
news in the background. There was yet another report that a White
girl originally described as missing was found dead. The report went
on to include a discussion on other missing White women. The
question asked was "Why do some who are missing receive more
attention from the media and more police resources than others?"
The reporter stated that many believe that race and/or class played a
major role. The President of the National Association of Journalists
confirmed that there have been studies to support the fact that young
White women receive more media attention and police assistance
than any other group. It's true that in the United States of America,
the police, hired to serve and protect, can decide which lives are more
valuable than others.

At one point during the last few years or so, it seemed that we
were searching for a White woman or her killer every week. These
stories were reported with great urgency, even though the general
public was not in imminent danger. One could change the station to
another major network and each featured the same in-depth story on
the same missing woman. I knew them by name: Natalee Hollaway,
Imet Sanguein, and Lacey Peterson. I didn't know the names of those
Black women who were missing. I happened to learn about those
women through conversations with a friend or colleague. There was
the pregnant girlfriend of professional football player, Ray Caruth,

whom he was convicted of killing. Also, there was the Hunter College student who disappeared while on spring break in Miami. A pregnant woman from Philadelphia went missing around the same time Natalee Hollaway disappeared. Finally, a college student from New York was tortured for days before she was brutally murdered. None of these stories were reported with the same urgency as were the reports related to the White victims.

It saddens me to know that my sisters were either missing or had their lives taken violently and their stories were not worth reporting by mainstream media. I knew that it was not because they were not as wealthy or famous as the White establishment attempts to portray but because they were Black, and the lives of Black women are not valued.

History reminds us that Black women were treated as sexual objects by White men and used by White women to care for their children; so it is not surprising to me that the importance of our lives are discounted. However, what is alarming is the fact that we as Black people are not outraged by this injustice. If not our men, then we Black women should be more vocal, particularly because we could be the next victims, as could our mothers, sisters, daughters or friends. We must be proactive rather than reactive.

As I became more cognizant of the grim reality of the fate of missing Black women, I began to pay close attention to the news coverage as offered by major networks and cable television. I reviewed the local and national news, in addition to shows by Oprah and Nancy Grace. Even though the topics discussed on the Oprah Winfrey show feature more than missing persons, I expected more coverage on missing Black women.

Nancy Grace, on the other hand, hosts a show on cable television that focuses on to the disappearance and murder of women and children. Most of the air time is dedicated to stories about White women and children. In order to confirm my theory, I monitored the Nancy Grace show each day over a six-month period. I reviewed and documented each case she discussed. My findings were as follows: Ms. Grace chose to highlight those crimes that had an impact on people with whom she could relate. She stated on several occasions that the victims could have been her mother, sister, children or friends. The misfortune is that we as Black folks do not utilize our positions of power as a platform to safeguard our own neighborhoods. We have been trained to concentrate our efforts on the betterment of the White establishment and to abandon the practice most necessary to the progression of our community—**cohesion.**

I often think about the young Black woman whose lifeless body was found in the trunk of my neighbor's car. Her identity was unknown. There was no plea from the Passaic County Sheriff's Department or the Prosecutor's Office to locate her killer. There was no coverage on the nightly news but rather a paragraph in the local paper several days later.

While watching crime television, I learned about a Black man in Bakersfield, California who killed his wife and three young children (the youngest only six weeks old) in 2003. This was a story of which I was not familiar and do not remember it as a high profile case such as the "Lacey Peterson" story.

I am concerned as a Black woman and mother of a beautiful little girl that if either she or I were missing, our safe return would not be newsworthy, as our lives are not worth saving in the eyes of the White media or the Black community.

LOVE,
AFRICAN-AMERICAN STYLE

"The personal and intimate relations between
African-American men and women dates back to Africa
where they were clearly defined, traditional roles for men
and women. These roles were obliterated by the cruel
economics of slavery."
Anderson J. Franklin, PhD—Author

Similar to women of other cultures, African-American women hope to find a mate with whom they will spend the rest of their lives. While one may think that this journey is a simple one, any random African-American woman will confirm that this is the furthest from the truth. The issues that face the African-American community have a direct impact on Black on Black monogamy and marriage.

Dating

By the time a Black female turns fifteen or sixteen, she will begin to notice that her Black male counterpart has begun to show interest in women of other races, particularly White women. This reality becomes more prominent once entering into college.

Let me begin with the most recent televised proposal of a handsome young Black professional football player who asked his red-head, White girlfriend to marry him. This televised presentation occurred during the Super Bowl which is the most watched television event in the country. It was a statement loud and clear and we sisters got it. Our successful and professional Black men are choosing love with women other than their own, a practice that they learn very early in life. Let's revisit the story of Yuri Wright, the high school football star was expelled from the Catholic High School in New Jersey due to sexual comments on his twitter page. The most memorable comment "I'm gonna' marry a bad White Bitch!" I'm sure it was that statement which resulted in his expulsion.

I discussed this disturbing situation with my fifteen-year-old son who is intelligent, handsome, and exhibits some athletic talent. I explained that young Yuri has based his idea of beauty and success on the White view of the world, adopted by many Black men. He didn't say "I'm going to marry a bad woman" no matter the race but rather one who was "White." I went on to explain that clearly, no one has informed this young fool about the world in which he was eventually going to have access. It would be due only to his athletic ability that a White father would accept him to marry his beautiful White daughter. He doesn't realize that he's like property-similar to slavery. It's not uncommon for Black athletes to marry the daughters or relatives of high ranking athletic officials so when she gets rid of him all of his financial assets will go back to daddy. Finally, no one told him that when he marries that "bad White bitch" that he better keep her, because when it's time to go in front of the White judge there will be a price to pay for marrying this beautiful White woman in the first place.

The reality is that many Black men are choosing to marry outside of their race at alarming rates. It's not only White women with whom they are seeking partnership, but Hispanic and Asian women as well. According to my male sources, brothers have been traveling to the Dominican Republic, Brazil, and other islands searching for love. While they not only find these women to be physically superior to Black women, they also believe them to be more submissive. One sister told me how she saw a male friend walking with his new Dominican woman as though she were Halle Berry. While she described the woman as "attractive" she went on to say that she could not even speak English and he did not speak Spanish. The message from the brother was "I would rather be with a woman with whom I cannot communicate then to be with you (sister) and your big mouth!"

The Attitude

According to my many male sources, Black men have discovered that life is more enjoyable and less stressful without their female counterpart. It has been explained to me that women of other races are more attentive and seem to understand their role in the relationship. Black women are extremely combative and no man wants to battle the white man all day only to arrive home to a woman who is cold and argumentative. While I sympathize with my brothers, I believe that this dilemma is two-fold. Somewhere along the line during our tragic history, things went very wrong between African-American men and women. The genuine respect, attraction, and need to protect their queen no longer exist. If you are a Black woman and live in the Tri-state area (New York, New Jersey, and Connecticut) Black men may not acknowledge your presence when walking by or entering a room. Nevertheless, some sisters no longer view the Black man as her king but rather another dependent or a "man-child."

It's alarming that anytime Black women gather socially, whether in a small group or one that's larger, the topic of discussion seems to take focus on Black men—whether you have one, can't find one, or don't want the one that you have. Those who are single seem to feel that Black men are considering women of other races as well as those who are much younger. However, those in relationships with Black men feel as though their mates are too weak to run the household, leaving them to fill their shoes. This issue I do understand as it was my own, however, I do know that there are some brothers who are competent but have chosen women who are not appreciative of them. Most of my most unpleasant experiences in business and personal have been with sisters. Their angry demeanor and uncooperative attitude during a disagreement is indescribable. Their inflated ego and need to control *every* situation whether their own or not is unattractive—not to mention scary. During numerous meetings with Black couples regarding their failure to abide by my rules or the behavior of their child, it's *always* the woman whose conduct is questionable. Oftentimes, the husband is clearly embarrassed as he cannot even reel her in.

Marriage

According to western culture, the institution of marriage is an established law that enables the legal, monogamous union of a man and a woman.

African-Americans assimilated into this cultural practice even though historically speaking marriage in Africa permitted men to be married to more than one woman. Some will argue that it is due to this practice that African-American men have an appetite for polygamy. This theory may be accurate, but African-American men should also understand that Africans who accepted this practice of polygamy provided equally for all of their women. A skill not adopted by our African-American men. This is a problem that has an impact on African-American women as we are marrying with the belief that our men will be faithful and committed.

Those who have experienced marriage will agree that the coupling of a man and woman with children and household responsibilities is not easy. Unfortunately, it's in hindsight and several years into a marriage that many of us question our decision to enter into such a permanent contract. While women oftentimes remain loyal in an unhappy marriage, men will not. In fact, they will stray when a marriage *is* stable.

Over generations, African-American women have learned and accepted the free-spirited habits of African-American men. Our mothers and grandmothers have reminded us that "men will be men" and that we should be happy that we have someone at all since there are so many Black women without a mate. In addition to this deficient advice, they also reminded us that promoting sex and sexuality was not lady like. We were not taught to take care of our men, both sexually and emotionally. Many of us thirty, forty, and fifty-something who were raised in a household with a mother and a father never witnessed intimacy between our parents.

We are all sexual beings and there is nothing submissive about wanting to please your partner. Men are visual creatures—women should keep that in mind when walking around the house in baggy clothing and a rag on their heads. However, we must be warned that the woman could be the most attentive mate and he may still wander. According to a group of African-American men during an informal discussion, they get tired of the same woman. So the reality is those who are going to continue on with African-American men, must be prepared to share. Either you can assume the role as wife or mistress—we must evolve and rethink our approach to relationships.

PRESIDENT BARACK OBAMA

"They want to ensure that he is a one term president.
They can't accept that an African-American is the head of
the number one country in the world."
Les Payne—Journalist

I have never witnessed more debate within the Black community than when Senator Barack Obama was nominated as a candidate for the office of President of United States of America.

While many were in support of his candidacy, some were not. It seemed that those most critical were Black men. I was troubled that my brothers did not acknowledge Senator Obama's contributions to the Black community as a young politician. It was bothersome that they did not feel that his integrity was genuine. Some were disappointed with his failure to respond with urgency to the victims of Hurricane Katrina. Another was the belief that that he was a puppet for White corporate America and that his election would not benefit Black people. The final group of men did not have any specific reason to not support Senator Obama. It's safe to say that those with no clear issue were envious of his celebrity in the world. They believed that there were others more qualified than Obama My question was "who?" Most of our Black male leaders are simply opportunists chasing the camera, looking for a photo opportunity.

As I discussed my concerns with a young educated brother from New Orleans, he reminded me that Obama's route to the Presidential candidacy bypassed the old Black boys' network. Those like Al Sharpton, Jesse Jackson, Charles Rangle, and Calvin Butts felt that Obama should have paid them homage during the planning stages of his campaign. Their approach to empowerment has been via the way of kickbacks and soul-selling, but Barack Obama was different. His credentials were heavy . . . accepted by White liberals. He didn't need to feed the sell-out machine as doing so would have been the demise of his Presidential campaign.

Young Obama

After college, Obama moved to the south side of Chicago. As he became involved in the arena of politics, he noticed the inequalities that faced this urban area. Young Obama realized that change was not going to come from the top but rather had to come from the bottom. He discovered that he needed to organize Black folks. There was a need to create a grassroots group that the citizens of this community would support and operate.

Obama met with a group of people from the neighborhood, mostly single Black mothers. He listened to their concerns and taught them how to identify the problems and then turn them into issues. The goal was to bring their concerns to the proper agencies. Obama's organization would develop projects to improve the community. He also met with Black ministers in the community to discuss gang violence, crime rate, and the need for job training programs. He was very organized and always facilitated meetings that had an agenda.

I understood the politics behind Senator Obama's candidacy, but I was not optimistic about his being able to win the most powerful seat in the land. I was not confident that members of the White establishment, cultivated for over four-hundred years, would readily accept a Black man in what they believed to be their White House. I didn't believe that our vote as Black people would be included. Whether or not it was, we will never know, because it is clear that his election would not have happened without the White vote.

Election Day

This was one of the most exciting mornings in our household. We followed the campaign process with our three children ages twelve, eight, and four. They understood that it was important for us to visit the voting site as a family on this historic day, for even if

Senator Obama were not elected, as he would be the first Black man considered for the Presidency.

Upon arriving at P.S. 26 in Paterson, New Jersey, we descended upon a parking lot full of people, an area that was normally empty on Election Day. This was the first day in my adult life that I was proud to be an American. We waited at the end of a line that wrapped around the building. These were my people of all shades and ages, from newborns to the elderly. The experience reminded me of images that I had seen as a child post-Jim Crow in the South, when Black people were murdered and brutalized fighting for their right to stand on such a line. The mood of the crowd was cheerful, but quiet. Many were not convinced that this process that we know as democracy was trustworthy. They were not sure that their vote would count, but it was worth taking the chance.

As we waited in line, people engaged in idle chatter. I spoke to college students as well as to former gang members who were voting for the first time. As we talked, one of the city's White politicians used this moment as a photo opportunity for himself. As he moved down the line shaking hands, Black folks were honored that he had acknowledged them. Disappointed with the passive ways of our people, I shook my head in disgust as he approached me. When he extended his hand, I declined a handshake and reminded him that he had never done anything for my community. I reminded him of the issues that had prompted me to contact him over a period of two years with no response. He and his camp moved away slowly with a look of shock and embarrassment. What a great day!

We waited in line for fifty minutes or so. Once inside the polling site, two of my three children participated in the electoral process by pulling the lever identified as "Barack Obama." Soon after, they both expressed concern about being late to school. I explained that learning can take place outside the classroom and that this historical day was a learning experience that they would not receive in the classroom of their Catholic school.

That evening, we decided to host an "election watch party." Eight couples and their children came to our home so that we could follow the results of the election. We all felt the need to be together. The teens chatted, the younger children played, and the adults ate and watched the coverage. As the time grew near, we all gathered in the den. All thirty-one of us sat quietly as we waited for the results of the last state to be read. Obama was victorious! Senator Obama was now the first Black President in the history of the country. We screamed, hugged, and even cried. I informed my children that they could now salute the American flag with pride.

As I drove through my predominately Black neighborhood, American flags were draped in front of most of the homes where they had never hung before. The statement was "CHANGE!" Nevertheless, I do understand that if the country were at its economic peak, White folks would not have given Obama the opportunity for the presidency.

Post Election

According to Dr. Joy DeGruy, clinical psychologist, Obama's position produces a sense of hope, but we must not underestimate the influence of the White supremacists who sit by quietly. She goes on to say that there are those who are angry that Obama is in office and have created a backlash that may not necessarily impact the President but has affected Black people on the streets. She describes these people as those who have been "dyed in the wool" of racism in this country. They are police officers, shop owners, or other business people who may use their level of authority to harass others.

Dr. DeGruy reminds us that President Obama's Presidency cannot change four hundred years of institutional racism and that we should not become complacent and believe that the fight is over.

The terroristic behavior towards members of President Obama's camp is to be expected, as those from the White Right can't accept the fact that a Black man with a vision has infiltrated their system of hate and corruption, a system that has plagued this country for over four hundred years. During a segment of *Like It Is* with the late Gil Noble, journalist Les Payne stated that "they" will do anything possible to ensure that his presidency is for only one term.

Two years after President Obama's election, Republican politicians and supporters profess their vow to "take back the country." I asked myself, "From where will they take it?" It's already been to hell and back. While I have always been aware of the fact that President

Obama would be expected to perform miracles from his first day in office, I am always disappointed that many brothers and sisters are so ignorant that they too fall into the trap. I have heard many describe our President as "incompetent." How could they not appreciate the President's efforts, whether effective or not? Success requires trial and error.

Sadly, those Black supporters who voted for the President in 2008 no longer support his campaign. Many have verbalized their disappointment with his efforts to assist working class people who have fallen victim to the economy. Not surprisingly, Black folks have responded with such dismay, as we are impatient and easily persuaded by others.

However, one conscious brother expressed his dissatisfaction with the President as he has ignored the increased rate of police brutality within the Black community. This brother, a retired Sergeant with the New York City Police Department, thought that as a Black man, President Obama would address the illegal behavior of those expected to protect and serve. If this discussion had taken place two years ago I would have disagreed with the brother, but to date, I must concur. I am disappointed with the lack of attention given to the injustices and discrimination towards Black people—particularly Black children. Nevertheless, I did not expect immediate *CHANGE* during the first term—I will continue to support the Obama Campaign—with *HOPE* that Mr. President will take a stand for *HIS* people.

CONCLUSION

The definition of community has been defined as: The group with whom people can gather to focus on cultural and political issues as it affects them. Most critical to the mobility of any group of people is a feeling of pride, community, and a clear understanding of contributions and obstacles as faced by their ancestors. Embracing one's culture provides each member with a foundation on which to build. Doing so creates a sense of loyalty and the need to participate in the effort to lift up and to protect the group. Unfortunately, this is not a philosophy assumed by most Black folks, creating a dilemma within the Black culture. We have chosen to assimilate within the dominant culture rather than embrace and celebrate our own heritage, as so many other cultures do.

Living as Black in the United States of America has an impact on the daily lives of **all** Black people, whether one is cognizant of the effects or not. Our failed community and its schools have caused distress among a population of Black children, particularly males. If we don't believe in them, who will? Our failure to advocate for our children has left some feeling a sense of hopelessness and has resulted in the loss of inner-strength and any real sense of self-worth—leading to destructive behavior.

The deficit within our community has debilitated our culture as African people. The structural breakdown post Civil Rights movement was the beginning of the end of an era. The focus became "me and mine" rather than "us and we." There were no more demands for civil rights because many believed that their rights were honored—experiencing a false sense of security and becoming a people displaced. Black people were now afforded the "American dream." Approved for mortgages, loans, and credit cards, they now had access to possessions and situations denied to them in the past. The conspiracy to denigrate and to control Black folks would be successful. The distraction of material items would cloud our ability to respond to the influx of drugs and crime filtering into our neighborhoods. As we saturated the economy with our purchases of homes, cars, clothing, jewelry and other luxury items, it would not be parallel to our economic power. Pseudo-activists (leading Blacks) would begin to position themselves in major cities across the country—traitors who would contribute to our downward spiral. Members of the dominant culture were aware of the disloyalty among the "leading Blacks," utilizing this information to infiltrate accordingly.

The conspiracy to suppress Black folks did not just occur. This plan began with the atrocities of the North American Slave Trade, a period in history when African people were stolen from their land and forced to build another, for people who would commit heinous crimes against them while enjoying the fruits of their labor. The spirit of the African male would be broken. His manhood would be challenged and his confidence and respect for self would diminish. This period would mark the beginning of the breakdown of the African-American family—and we would not recover.

Black folks never learned how to survive as an ethnic group in a capitalistic society. Sadly, I am not hopeful that we can achieve cohesiveness comparable to what we had pre-civil rights—we are too far gone. The three reasons are the following:

- Culturally speaking, there are probably more different groups of Black people than any other race, resulting in more focus on our differences than on our similarities. No matter how we view one another (African-American, African, Haitian, West Indian) other people view us as and treat us the same way because of the color of our skin. This alone should bind us, as we are all fighting the same fight, even though some of us are more conscious of the injustices than others are. Cruise (1984) suggests that the political, economic and cultural components be identified and fused into one political agenda for a "progressive Black culture."
- From a socio-economic standpoint, we span the spectrum, most of us in the middle or at the bottom. There are the socially and economically deprived who may be the third or fourth generation to be born into poverty, with no resources

to break the cycle. Then there are upper-middle-class Black folks who believe that they are superior to their economically deprived counterparts—feeling no sense of sympathy for their struggles. Finally, there are the affluent that are so far removed from the life experiences encountered by the others that they do not feel the effects directly of the social inequalities and hardships. Surprisingly, many wealthy Black folks were born and raised in lower- or middle-income households, realizing their fortune as athletes or entertainers.

We will never gain economic strength in The United States, for we have no foundation or support system. Black people live according to the premise that "I can't support my Black brethren because he may surpass me economically." In addition, non-African-American Black folks believe that the rule of consumerism in the United States is to spend money with White businesses.

• Finally, there are too many Black folks under the spell of the establishment as they have accepted the belief that their lives and those of their family members are not as valuable as are the lives of their White counterparts. This is a fact, as there are no long-term demands when our men and children are brutalized and murdered at the hands of the police. There are no long-term demands when our children are mistreated and mis-educated in school. There are no long-term demands when our children and women are missing and there is no local or national exposure comparable to the response of the disappearance of White women and children.

Instead of focusing our energy on how to obtain the respect rightfully deserved, we continue to be most critical of one another—a practice quite evident since the election of President Obama. Each month more brothers and sisters profess their disapproval of the President's effectiveness. Rather than support his efforts to make a difference in a nation that has been corrupt since its inception, we take the side of the establishment that expected change on the first day of President Obama's Presidency. It wouldn't surprise me if

Obama's election was a set-up by both the Left and the Right. The plot could have been planned in this way:

- Here we have a country that is in turmoil. What better time to put a Negro in office but now? Once in office, the Negro will be unable to produce enough change in a manner of time acceptable to the public, thus resulting in the people's choice to NEVER put another Negro in office again.

Rebuilding the Black community seems virtually impossible. Doing so would require the organization of a mass movement that would include a point person from every major city in the country. These brothers and sisters would have to be young, conscientious, and motivated. The team would have to prepare a paradigm that would address all of the issues discussed in this document.

To begin, the team would have to identify and exclude the current gatekeepers and leading Blacks. A panel of elders would be created for support only. This group would have to understand and accept the vision of the team without taking over.

After the model is in place, there will be a town hall meeting in each city—with a point person at the helm. People from the community would have to participate and accept the vision while also assuming a role on the team. The agenda would be "taking back Black." The members from the community would be considered foot soldiers. The point people will be considered foot soldiers with administrative positions.

Too often we have accepted the notion that expressing feelings of anger towards the establishment for the mistreatment of our family members and children make us "angry Blacks." Anger is indeed a true emotion. If someone hurts you, it's natural to say "that hurts." We have taught our children to turn the other cheek—thus resulting in a generation of young people who do not know how to channel their natural feelings of anger because we have convinced them that it is unnecessary to do so.

The issues of police brutality within the Black community have become commonplace in cities around the country. The practice is the manifestation of the hatred towards Black men. It's safe to say that physical abuse at the hands of the police is likely to cause mental anguish for the victim. The ability to cope is a skill-set that we do not consider when viewing the youngest victim. There is clearly an emotional process through which one moves in a situation when he is being brutalized at the hand of someone with such power. How can we expect our children to comprehend and survive effectively such a dehumanizing experience when an adult would be unable to do so?

Our children are our future and we are not preparing them for the journey on which White America will attempt to take them. It is possible for more of our children to succeed in this White racist society, but only with the assistance of their elders.

"My President is still Black"
6 Novemebr 2012

AFTER THOUGHTS

On Friday, December 2, 2011 I was awakened by an unexplained feeling of nausea and discomfort. Upon arriving to work, I complained to my employees that I was feeling ill, and they teased that maybe I was expecting. I continued through my morning only to be halted by a phone call that would forever change my life.

My ex-husband and father of my three children was found dead in his home from an apparent heart attack. How would I tell my two sons and daughter that their forty-eight-year-old father was dead—particularly since six months earlier, his mother (their maternal grandmother to whom they were extremely close) passed away from cancer.

The conversation would be like no other. My heart raced as I felt the onset of a panic attack. Once the devastating news was delivered, my fifteen-year-old son asked several times "You mean he's just not living anymore? He's not alive?" He then went into a state of shock for the next few hours. My six-year-old insisted, "You mean Pop-Pop died, not Da-Da." I went on to repeat myself and say no "Da-Da" your father, died. In her mind it made more sense that her eighty-year-old grandfather, who was ill, would pass on before her father did. During this entire dialogue, my eleven-year-old son sat in silence, as he remains today.

One month later, reality has set in. Friends and family have returned to their normal routine, and both the doorbell and the telephone have stopped ringing. I have been forced to think about my life and the choices that I have made over the last few years. I admitted to myself that while I was shocked and saddened by my ex-husband's death, I was not surprised. Five years ago ALLAH provided me a path to follow—one that would prepare me for the future. He provided me with a sense of strength, commitment, and consciousness to be able to effectively raise three little Black children in a society that will not be so kind.

My goal for *The Black Papers* is to present the series of events that I believe have interfered with the healthy growth and progression of Black people from slavery to the election and re- election of the first African-American President. My personal experiences have influenced the content, but it is the death of my children's father that refines my feelings about Black people.

The way in which we operate our household and raise our children is most fundamental to our existence. While many successful adults have come from single parent households, the most ideal situation is a Black home with both a father and a mother—he who has something to offer, and she who allows him to do so. If both parents understand their roles and work as a unit to prepare their children to function as productive citizens while teaching the children the importance of community, we as a people would do more than thrive. We would prosper then conquer, but there is an obstacle.

We Black mothers have continued to impede such progression by our fascination with our boys. We spoil them to no end, and oftentimes, if there is a male head of household, we interfere as he attempts to discipline and guide them. We become so enamored with their being that we lose sight of the fact that one day they will become heads of household in their own homes, but that they will be unable to fulfill their obligations because they are too weak to do so. As they move through life with their mothers as their crutch, they wither away—loved to death.

SELECETED BIBLIOGRAPHY

Ball, H.ADefiantLife:ThurgoodMarshall. NewYork:CrownPublishing, 1998.

Banks, W. Black Intellectuals. New York: WW Norton & Company, 1996.

Beals, M. Warriors Don't Cry. New York:Washington Square Press, 1994.

Beauchamp, K. "The Injustice Files." At the End of the Rope. Documentary 2012.

Bell, D. Faces at the Bottom of the Well. New York: Basic Books, 1992. Berliner, D. & Biddle,/b. The Manufactured Crisis, Myths, Fraud, and

the Attack On America's Public Schools. New York: Addison-Wesley Publishing Company, 1995.

Blassingame, J.W. The Slave Community. New York: Oxford University Press. 1979.

Boyd-Franklin, N. and Franklin, A. J. Boys into Men: Raising Our African American Teenage Sons. New York: Plume, 2000.

Booth, K. "American Drug War: The Last White Hope" documentary, 2007.

Carmichael. H. C. Black Power, the Politics of Liberation in America. New York: Vintage Books, 1967

Comer, J. Waiting for a Miracle. New York: Penguin Books, 1997.

Cruise, Harold. The Crisis of the Negro Intellectual. New York: Quill Books, 1984.

Dubois, W.E.B. The Education of Black People. New York: Monthly Review Press. 1973. Ellison, R. Invisible Man. New York: Penguin Books. 1952

Carson, C. Civil Rights Chronicle. Illinois: Legacy Publishing. 2003. Fanon, F. Black Skins, White Masks. New York:Monthly Review,

1967. Franklin, A.J. From Brotherhood to Manhood. New Jersey: John Wiley & Sons 2004.

Franklin, J.H. The Color Line. Missouri: University of Missouri Press. 1993.

Freire, P. Teachers as Cultural Workers. Colorado: Westview Press. 1998.

Gates, L. The African-American Century New York: Simon & Schuster, 2000.

Grant, C. Negro With a Hat. New York: Oxford Press.

Hamilton, C.V. Adam Clayton Powell Jr. New York: Collier Books 1991.

Harper, H. Letters to a Young Brother. New York: Penguin Books, 2006.

Herrnstein, R. and Murray, C. The Bell Curve. _____() Hooks, B. Killing Rage. New York: Owl Book, 1995.

Hughes, L. A Pictorial History of Black Americans. New York: Crown Publishers, 1983.

Kennedy, R. Sellout. New York: Vintage Books, 2009

Kozol, J. Savage Inequalities: Children In American Schools. New York: Harper Collins, 1992.

Kunjufu, J. Countering the Conspiracy to Destroy Black Boys: Vol. I. Chicago: African American Images. 1983.

Lott. S.K. The Truth About American Slavery. South Carolina: Eastern Digital Resources, 2004.

Marable, M. Malcolm X. New York: Viking Books, 2011. Noble, G. "Like It Is." Dr. Joy DeGruy. 2011. Noble, G. "Like It Is." Les Payne 2011.

Rich, F. The Greatest Story Ever Sold. New York: Penguin Group, 2006. Washington Post 2002 and Washington Post 2012.

Weatherford J. Indian Givers: How Native Americans Transformed the World. New York: Three Rivers Press, 2010

Webb, G. Dark Alliance. New York: Seven Stories Press, 1999.

Woodson, C. The Mis-Education of Black People. Washington D.C.: Africa World Press, 1999.

PEACE

AND

PROGRESS!

www.ingramcontent.com/pod-product-compliance
Lightning Source LLC
Chambersburg PA
CBHW020259290526
45784CB00003B/1300